"Every playw[...] [...]ienne Kennedy's
shadow, full s[...]

—ᴰᴿᴬᴺᴰᴱᴺ Jacobs-Jenkins

"He Brought Her Heart Back in a Box is small, brief, gnomic, and darkly mysterious . . . Welcome to the mind of Adrienne Kennedy, the poet who refracts all of world history and its attendant cultural artifacts through the prism of the American shame, racism, and the personal agonies it has visited on generations of individuals . . . Every line of Kennedy's speech is drenched in blood and tears, and toil and sweat are never far from its surface. The effect is unnerving and dizzying, guaranteed—as Kennedy's plays are always guaranteed—to trouble the mind for weeks on end."

—Michael Feingold, *Village Voice*

"Adrienne's language transports the reader into the vibrating consciousness of a woman whose heart we can feel beating and whose mind we feel branching poetically from her core. *He Brought Her Heart Back in a Box* is a landscape of the mind—unconventionally aligning people, places, things, and time periods in a dreamlike fashion, never taking a straight path from one event to another if a more beautiful route is available. It's a wandering, time-traveling, ecstatic celebration of internal life and the poetics of the mind. And it is a testament to the universal empathy that arises from the seeds of extreme specificity of experience."

—Natalie Portman

"One of the American theater's greatest and least compromising experimentalists . . . Kennedy's dramas are sites of living history, where personal stories of racism's unhealed wounds mingle with dark tales thieved from the Brothers Grimm and 1940s Hollywood."

—Ben Brantley, *New York Times*

"Adrienne Kennedy's work is a lighthouse, a liberating beacon reminding me that no structure, no mode of expression or subject matter is off limits to me as a dramatist."

—Aleshea Harris

"Kennedy is an American avant-garde master ... *He Brought Her Heart Back in a Box* is small and slippery, consisting of onion-skin strata: literary references, cinematic echoes, and long runs of remembered (or invented) family history. It's simultaneously dense and feather light—the surface is a made-for-the-movies tragic romance, full of wistfulness and charm, yet below lies layer after layer of American violence ... Watching it is like sitting next to the playwright as she points to photographs, mixing stories from her favorite films with tales from her family's past ... It has a way of slipping into the far back of your mind. After a week, you'll be able to imagine that it was whispered to you, or even that you made it up yourself. It only took me a day before I dreamed of the green glass box. It was then I felt I'd seen the show for real."

—HELEN SHAW, *4COLUMNS*

"While many of Ms. Kennedy's inferiors received top prizes for blame-the-victim literature and theater, she came up with *Sleep Deprivation Chamber* (with son Adam P. Kennedy) in 1996. In my opinion, this play is one of the most powerful indictments of the racist criminal-justice system yet penned ... Black writers like Adrienne Kennedy are not there to coddle, or to comfort. They challenge us. They contest official lies. For them, truth is more important than a dubious fame, and they are willing to offend white nationalists whether they be present in politics or culture."

—ISHMAEL REED

"Whenever I encounter an Adrienne Kennedy play, it explodes my brain and challenges me in ways that I dream of my own work doing to others ... There are not many artists who when mentioned an almost silent reverence is heard. Her voice changes the molecules of the theater space like none other and has been a beacon to me as I continue to find my own."

—ROBERT O'HARA

"A true poet of the theater, Adrienne's incantatory mixture of myth, personal experiences, and delight in language has created an individual and indelible body of work."

—MICHAEL KAHN

He Brought Her Heart
Back in a Box

—

and Other Plays

He Brought Her Heart Back in a Box

and Other Plays

Adrienne Kennedy

THEATRE COMMUNICATIONS GROUP
NEW YORK
2020

Contents

Foreword

By Margo Jefferson

A drienne Kennedy makes intricate, incandescent art from the charged materials of our family, racial, sexual, and psychological lives. Intimate secrets and desires unfold on vast cultural landscapes. A day in a single life becomes a day that will live in historical infamy. The spaces that contain her plays are haunted. Public or private—houses, museums, theaters, parks, train stations—they have witnessed life, death, and every kind of passion. They contain memories that can't be plastered over, rerouted or torn down. That's why, even on the page, her stage directions are like site-specific artworks.

Kennedy titled her wonderful 1987 collage-memoir *People Who Led to My Plays*. But "people" has many meanings in her lexicon. "People" are whatever humans, animals, objects, art works, and ideas take root in her mind. They include her parents Etta and C. W. Hawkins, her brother Cornell Kennedy, and her sons Adam and Joe; they include Malcolm X, Beethoven, Queen Victoria, Charlotte and Emily Brontë, Gwendolyn Brooks; *Beowulf* and Grendel's mother, *Dracula*, and *Frankenstein*; jazz and pop stars from Nat Cole to John Lennon; cruel, predatory policemen; luminous Hollywood actors (especially Bette Davis). "People" are owls and rats, statues, and postcards. They include the words of Virgil and Frantz Fanon; of spirituals and Tin Pan Alley songs; reinventions of Mary Shelley and Anna Karenina. And always— narrating, watching, dreaming with and for us—are complex, charismatic Black women writers, absent on theater stages for so many centuries.

Everything has its double and its shadow in Kennedy's plays. The past is always present. What's suppressed or unspoken always seeks and finds a language. It can be the language of dreams. It can be sudden violent action. But thoughts and emotions don't simply lead to actions they *are* actions. "My plays are meant to be states of mind," she has written.

States of mind know no borders, no boundaries. And her language knows none. It is explosive and visceral, fine-spun and elegiac. Grand and formal: one hears Roman and Biblical cadences; one hears the long line of the sorrow songs. Lyric and sensuous: one hears Romantic and Surrealist poetry.

> He understands history. He understands the devastation of the human spirit.

Those harsh words, a kind of death sentence, describe the murderous white Southern patriarch in *He Brought Her Heart Back in a Box*. Kennedy renders the corruption of the human spirit with unblinking precision. She also cherishes the solace, the succor that art provides. Art is a talisman in the lives of her people, often the only power they can trust. It can't always save their lives, but it can redeem them. The play's doomed, vibrant young lovers, Kay and Chris, find each other through Noël Coward's operetta *Bitter Sweet*. The enchantment of its words and music on stage and screen gives them the imaginative courage they need to cast off the racist cruelties that have maimed their families for generations and seek a life together. Their valor matters as much as the brutality that engulfs them.

He Brought Her Heart Back in a Box is a romance, a history play, and a revenge tragedy. *Etta and Ella* is a charged gothic New York tale—part narrative thriller and part play. The narrative builds through an intricate collection of image-clues; the play layers dialogue, monologue, and voiceover; a single scene can amount to what feels like an eternity:

> A deserted wing of Yeshiva School faced Riverside Drive where abandoned children hid. Shattered steps led to a yard of stones and weeds. Etta sat on the steps and wrote:

> someone will be murdered

Etta and her sister Ella are brilliant Black scholars and writers. They are driving each other to a breaking point. Like conjoined twins forced to share food and space, they've shared ambitions and material for years, fictionalizing and cannibalizing each other's lives. Can they separate and survive or must they destroy each other?

Mom, How Did You Meet The Beatles? is a tender, rueful portrait of Kennedy as an innocent abroad in 1960s London. She's there to adapt *In His Own Write*, John Lennon's charming book of stories, poems, and drawings. And with ironic hindsight, we could also call this play, which takes the form of an interview with Kennedy by her son Adam, "In *Her* Own Write." That write/right seems inalienable when she first arrives. She's a successful, experimental American playwright. Adapting Lennon's fancy-free word-wizardry is a perfect fit. But in this coterie of powerful, celebrated, and closely connected Englishmen, her claim to her own idea slips away. Let me use the past tense. It slipped away then. Here and now in these pages, with Adam acting as documentarian and alter ego, she finds a bittersweet happy ending by reclaiming and restaging her story.

What an exhilarating range of styles and genres these three works display. Each claims new imaginative territory. Each invents a new cultural geography. Adrienne Kennedy is a great American explorer and artist.

New York City
July 2020

MARGO JEFFERSON is a Pulitzer Prize–winning cultural critic. She is the author of *Negroland: A Memoir* (Penguin Random House, 2015).

He Brought Her Heart
Back in a Box

He Brought Her Heart Back in a Box had its world premiere at Theatre for a New Audience (Jeffrey Horowitz, Founding Artistic Director; Dorothy Ryan, Managing Director; Michael Page, General Manager) in New York, on January 18, 2018. It was directed by Evan Yionoulis. The scenic design was by Christopher Barreca, the costume design was by Montana Levi Blanco, the lighting design was by Donald Holder, the original music and sound design were by Justin Ellington, the video design was by Austin Switser; the dramaturg was Jonathan Kalb, and the production stage manager was Cole Bonenberger. The cast was:

KAY	Juliana Canfield
CHRIS/HARRISON AHERNE	Tom Pecinka

Images

TRAIN CARS
Dark, passing WHITE/COLORED stations.

NEW YORK THEATER
Small like old Amato Opera House.

STAGE
Opera backdrop.

BACKSTAGE
Dressing room.
Table, chair, mirror.

SCHOOL
Kay enters from beyond; near her is a long, long, staircase, dark.
She is pretty, fragile, pale.
Watches play through an opening that leads to the stage.

Music

The song "See See Rider Blues" runs throughout the play.
It is the motif of this world.
The Ma Rainey version I heard as a child, summers in Georgia.

Place

Montefiore, Georgia.

June 1941.

Outside the town a boarding school for colored.

School play, *The Massacre at Paris*, is in progress.

Characters

HARRISON AHERNE

Chris's father.

KAY

Very pretty, student, seventeen.

When not in school she lives with her grandmother, a servant for people who run the town's canning factory.

They live in the center of the colored district in a decent house bought for her by the canning family.

CHRIS

Handsome, seventeen.

Working in a building adjacent to the school storeroom and office.

Office belongs to Harrison Aherne, white, one of the founders of the school.

Chris is his son.

Chris and Kay have known each other all their lives.

The town has less than six hundred people.

Chris lives with his parents in a house right on the edge of town.

His father, Harrison Aherne, is a landowner and businessman, and architect of the town's segregation.

Chris's mother, originally from Oglethorpe, has just died.

People see each other constantly on Main Street.

The people are all somehow connected.

Kay's father was a white writer of history and mystery. Her mother, who shot herself in the head when Kay was a baby, was colored. Her name was Mary.

Kay's father, who lived in nearby Oglethorpe, saw Mary most of the time when she helped her mother and he was a visitor at the canning family, the Walkers.

Kay's mother, Mary, was fifteen, striking and quiet.

The school play, The Massacre at Paris, *is in progress.*

Kay at the top of the stairwell can see through to the stage, hear clearly, see vague motion.

Down this long, long dark stairwell is a door.

Kay watches the play.

We hear voices.

On the walls of the school's corridor are drawings of Dante.

From the stage The Massacre at Paris:

The children of the boarding school are all colored.

The students in the play are about twelve to seventeen.

7

They say the lines accordingly:

Although my downfall be the deepest hell
For this I wake when others think I sleep
For this I wait that scorns attendance else
For this my quenchless thirst . . . whereon I Build

Hath often pleaded kindred to the King
For this, this head this heart this hand and sword
Contrives, imagines, and fully executes

Matters of import aimed at by many

Yet understood by none

For this hath heaven engendered me of earth.

The students do not try to make meaning of this play, it was assigned to them to perform.

Their courses of study are carefully monitored by the mayor's committee, although the headmaster is colored . . .

Headmaster Roseboro is a young Negro who graduated from Morehouse, a man who is dedicated to his students and has the burden of negotiating with the mayor's committee, who is white.

The lines read by the students are barely understandable.

The Massacre at Paris was chosen for unknown reasons by Harrison Aherne.

Kay watches the motion on the stage and listens.

The play continues from the stage:

My noble son and Princely Duke of Guise,
Now have we got the fatal straggling deer

Within the compass of a deadly toil
And as we late decreed, we may perform.

Though gentle minds should pity others' pains

Yet will the wisest note their proper grieves
And rather seek to scourge their enemies,
Than be themselves base subjects to the whip.

They repeat softly.

The door of the storeroom opens revealing the interior: clusters of panoramic photos, maps, drawings, letters on a dark wall, as well as piles of old books, large WHITE/COLORED signs, old desks, a radio, and two train cars, one designed for white people, one a Jim Crow car.

The dark interior is lit by kerosene lamps.

Barely visible is an old rolltop desk, a chair in the corner, and a replica of Montefiore, Georgia. The most dominant feature of the replica is Main Street and the ornate water fountain in the center of town, a white side and a colored side. Emphasized on the far left of the replica is the red brick train station, and positioned in the miniature waiting rooms more signs WHITE/COLORED.

From the open door and ascending the steps comes Chris Aherne, good-looking, light brown thick hair, tall, very blue eyes. His skin is pale . . . despite the Georgia sun. He spends many hours indoors reading; practicing songs, monologues; and writing and drawing. He wants to leave Georgia and go on the stage in New York, which he is about to do.

This is the day he and his father have just buried his mother. As he ascends the staircase he never takes his eyes off Kay.

There is no doubt that they are quite drawn to each other.

Muffled passages from The Massacre at Paris *are heard.*

CHRIS

Good evening, Kay.

KAY

Evening, Mr. Chris.

He is white. She is not. He is still, in 1941, addressed with "Mr."

She looks toward the storeroom.

CHRIS

I'm doing a little work on the school books for my father. School will be out next week. He keeps close attention to the money the school spends.

Looks through to the stage.

Hears a passage from the play:

Those are my father's nigra children . . . the three on the end.

KAY

I know he comes to see them once or twice a year. They go down to Headmaster Roseboro's office to see him. He never walks on the grounds with them. But everyone knows Mr. Harrison Aherne is their father . . .

He watches the play.

Muffled lines are heard.

CHRIS

He built the Aherne Garden Cemetery for colored, for their mothers. He bought them tombstones. They are the only nigra women in Montefiore to have tombstones on their graves.

From the stage muffled lines are heard.

Kay, we buried my mother today. I've just come from Oglethorpe. That is where all her family is.

Kay is silent.

She used to say, "Christopher, your father loves those nigra children more than he does us. He buys them clothes almost as good as yours. He bought that girl of his a piano to play in that school." And my mother would sit in the sunroom and cry.

"But they aren't getting his peach orchards. I've seen to that. They cannot inherit a thing. I've seen to that. All these orchards will belong to you, Chris, when we are gone."

And she would cry and cry. Sometimes she would quote Robert E. Lee to me:

We must expect reverses even defeats. They are sent to teach us wisdom and prudence, to call forth greater energies, and to prevent our falling into greater disasters.

11

Pause.

Suddenly he says:

Shrewd tactics can win against superior armies.

That's Lee.

From the stage, the play continues.

He stares at Kay.

I saw you a while back at the movie house sitting up in the colored section.

KAY

Miss Lena, our teacher, took us.

CHRIS

It was *Bitter Sweet.* I used to see you all the time sitting under the weeping willow at your cousins on Aherne Road.

KAY

You and your father were on the way to the orchards. His chauffeur Austin would park the car and you and your father would get out and walk deep into the orchards.

CHRIS

His business was thriving then. He shipped peaches all up North. That was before the Depression. He's got money still but not as much. You know my grandfather practically built this town. He started the first bank.

KAY

What do you do down in the storeroom?

CHRIS

Just help out with school accounts and business. You know the building belongs to the county. My father is on the county board.

KAY

I heard Miss Pearl, your mother, died last Sunday.

CHRIS

(*Sudden*) Kay, I've been waiting for you. I knew you would be at the play. I want to talk to you.

KAY

My mother is dead too. When I was born she was ashamed of me. I was only five days old when she took the train to Cincinnati and left me in the country with her cousins until she could get on her feet.

She hoped to marry a boy from Montefiore who had lived down in the bottom in Montefiore and was now in Cincinnati. Robert, he had jobs fixing things: painting, plumbing jobs, and fixing electrical wiring. He had always loved Mary. He knew one day she was going to be a teacher. He wanted to buy a little house in Cincinnati.

My mother stayed with Maggie, Robert's aunt, who was half blind. She has been in Cincinnati since 1922. She and her husband had cooked for people until he died suddenly from heart trouble.

Maggie wrote me one time. She said, "Kay, your mother arrived in Cincinnati five days after your birth, her skin purple, she was covered in water from perspiration, the beautiful frail Mary. Her body had not healed yet. She was only fifteen.

"Robert and I tried to tend to her. But the noise of streetcars, the crowded apartment buildings, and there was always screaming from somewhere.

13

"She used to read the Bible to me.

"But in less than three weeks she was found dead in the freight elevator. They called me to come down to the basement.

"Your father and Harrison Aherne did just as they pleased with colored women. People were afraid of them.

"I still don't understand how she got in there. Kay, she had been stabbed to death. She was a sweet child and, Kay, I want you to know your mother loved you so much and as soon as she got well she was going to have Robert go and get you.

"Your grandmother was so mean to her. Mary had been living out in the country with her father's cousins the whole time she was carrying you. Her father, your grandfather, was a fine man. People say your grandmother was so mean it killed him. He used to preach all around Macon and Columbus, never had a church of his own.

"Old service elevator in the apartment. I loved Mary."

———

Light bright on storeroom, emphasis on WHITE/COLORED *sign and two train cars, one for white, and one a Jim Crow car. They stare down the stairwell into a room massively dark, yet illuminated by scores of photographs. A radio is heard a little now . . . war news.*

KAY

There are two train cars.

CHRIS

A smaller scale. My grandfather planned the Jim Crow car here: the straw seats, the small toilet, and the WHITE car velvet seats.

KAY

What is there?

It is dark and chaotic.

CHRIS

(Looking at chaos) The two train cars, a miniature of Montefiore, books.
Wilkie Collins, H.G. Wells, Shakespeare.
Baskets for packing peaches.
WHITE/COLORED signs.
There are old photographs of Berlin in 1934.
Roosevelt.
Helen Keller.
Extra kerosene lamps.
My father and me at tea in London on Maida Ave.
Textbooks.
Bucket and dipper.
Maps of southern Georgia.
Drawings and old photographs of town.

A huge drawing of the house my father was born in, a white wooden house with a few columns, three stories, sits far back from the road, built in 1860 by his father and now in 1941 has one usable room, the old parlor, and a kitchen. The rest of the house destroyed, fallen staircase, closed-up rooms, a very small front porch, drawing of colored side of town, blueprints, radio, and photos of Flint Farms built by the government.

Now he is quiet. They both are.

I'm going to leave for New York tomorrow, Kay. I'm never coming back. I want to go on the stage. I came here because I wanted to see you. I want to write to you. I want to marry you. We could run away and live in Paris after the war.

15

KAY

Just like in *Bitter Sweet*.

CHRIS

Yes.

KAY

Yes, I'll marry you, Chris.

———

Darkness, winter.

New York.

From his dressing room, stage beyond a set of Bitter Sweet, *Chris writes to Kay.*

CHRIS

I have been wondering who our German houseguests were when I was a child.

At night they went out walking. They carried blueprints and maps. One of them said to me, "You must be proud of your father, your family. Your grandfather practically built this town. He started the first bank.

"He has friends in London. He has friends who know Churchill.

"Your father is one of the biggest landowners in southern Georgia. Brilliant the way your grandfather divided this town; the placement of the WHITE/COLORED signs. He knew coloreds should not have paved roads, should not have tombstones, and should have to go to the post office to pick up their mail. Should be forbidden to try on clothing at Smith's Department Store.

"He just knew these things. He understands history. He understands the devastation of the human spirit.

"He knows the importance of making a person enter through the back door and of never addressing them as you are addressed. He understands how language can be used to humiliate."

KAY

(Writing from her room at Atlanta University) My grandmother always said we saw my father all the time on Main Street but he never looked our way.

Pause.

I am sending you photographs of our school lawns, our colors are pink and green and our football yell is, "Go Atlanta Go."

Pause.

My grandmother said, "I believe my daughter's heart was in a box he had. I believe he killed her and he might kill you.

"The way his mother would look at you.

"Your father would look away but *his* mother would look at you like she was going to kill you right there on Main Street.

"They say she told Mr. Aherne to get you into the boarding school, seeing you had made her very sick. Every time she came into town she saw you. And it had made her very sick and she was just happy her husband never lived to see his son's little nigger.

"Her son was such a disappointment. The Feltons are from aristocracy.

17

"She said: 'I told Charles that that nigger Mary was the devil. He had brought the devil into our lives.

"'I sent him to Chicago, but he came back. This wouldn't have happened if he weren't friends with Harrison. Harrison has always been crazy. He had a colored child by the time he was fifteen.

"'The Ahernes used to live out there in the country not on Main Street like we did.

"'And all those colored worked in the peach orchards that they owned.

"'Harrison had more money than Charles. He took Charles to Atlanta once. I used to tell him all the time if your father were alive he would kill you.

"'I'd hoped he was going to be a great writer. He wrote such beautiful stories when he was a boy . . . I didn't care much for those old mystery stories he wrote after he grew up. When he died they put one of his books on the main shelf of the library. Had that sunstroke and he was gone in a few days; only thirty-six.

"'Mamie, my cook, told me once, the colored people believe that Charles had something to do with that Mary's death. They always have believed that.'"

CHRIS

My father took me to Germany. In Berlin, they discussed the library on Main Street many times and how colored were strictly forbidden to enter. I was about ten years old when we took that trip.

———

December 1941.

New York City.

The stage of a small theater.

Chris sings four lines of "Dear Little Café," then goes backstage to the dressing room.

CHRIS
Kay, I'm sending you a book of Dylan Thomas poems.

Then the train cars come into view: Jim Crow and the WHITE car.

Chris remains backstage in darkness, to stage left is a stairwell.

Train cars moving.

Center stage: the two train cars.

Kay sits in the Jim Crow car, writing. In the WHITE car sits Harrison Aherne played by the same actor as Chris. He looks like his son, but older of course, wears a suit and panama hat. The resemblance to his son is intentional and has an artifice. He never takes his eyes off Kay.

Train cars bright.

Aherne never takes his eyes from Kay.

Music: Ma Rainey's "See See Rider Blues," and the same four lines from "Dear Little Café."

CHRIS'S VOICE
And I remember in Germany we stayed in a house on the Wannsee Lake. And my father took me to a parade.

Train cars bright, moving.

Since I have been in New York I think about Germany. My father always says he has many problems with his nigras. And I think what was he doing in Berlin? Why were we walking on Unter den Linden under the Brandenburg Gate?

No one is more patriotic than my father. He idolizes Roosevelt. He helped plan the government farms for colored, gave up part of his peach orchards and now he spends time working on the colored cemetery planting flowers.

He got your grandmother a job at Warm Springs.

Kay on train, train moves, Kay writes.

KAY

Chris.

No matter how many times I asked my grandmother she will never talk about my mother Mary—but . . . Maggie wrote me everything. It was Maggie who told me my mother shot herself. Whenever I would mention my mother, my grandmother would beat me with switches. "She went up yonder," she would say. "She went up yonder long ago."

Train dark.

CHRIS

(In dressing room) But it was my father who decided the colored should live at the bottom, the sunken part of town, reached by descending the road behind the church, the lowest level of the sandy roads.

Pictures on mirror.

In the evening I think of home, and in my dressing room have pictures of the train station, Main Street, the train ride coming into town beyond the fields of corn and sugar cane. Why were we in that house on the Wannsee Lake? My father designed a map of Montefiore for his friends and built a replica of the town. At night they walked along the lake. I heard them talking about the churches they belonged to.

Train and dressing room.

                                KAY

Chris.

Here are photos of my friends, my school colors, our school yell.

In dressing room, Chris stares.

Train moving.

My great-aunt, my grandmother's sister, talks all the time about the green box, all the time. "Your mother did not kill herself," she says. "She was killed and Maggie knows it. It was in the winter. I saw him with my own two eyes. Your father returned from up North with a green box—everybody saw it; it was a long glass box. Everybody said it had your mother's heart in it. We all saw it. He sat it in the center of the colored garden, the Aherne Garden.

"We all knew it was Mary's heart. Then it disappeared. Your father brought your mother's heart back in a box."

Darkness.

———

Backstage:

On the mirror: pictures of Kay; a ship; Dylan Thomas; still of movie, Invisible Man; *pictures from Kay at school lawn at Atlanta University; a program; ribbons of her school colors.*

Chris writes.

Music from the stage in the background. Chris is in the amateur production of Bitter Sweet.

CHRIS

I still, years later, see bodies of the baptized floating down the river, shot, because they had the ceremony too close to the land of Crackel Farm. The colored bodies . . . floating . . . only minutes before baptized in Jesus's name.

Pause.

Kay, I think of when I saw you at *Sun Valley Serenade.*

I watched you go up the steps to the colored benches. You had on a yellow dress.

Pictures of Kay on his mirror, illuminated.

Radio somewhere, war news.

Light on train cars.

Aherne has not moved, he stares at Kay, through the train cars. She writes to Chris.

Music: instrumental part of Ma Rainey's "See See Rider Blues" plays.

KAY

You were walking down the road with your father then disappeared into the aisles of sugar cane. I sat on the porch of my cousins and watched you. Inside the house they kept the radio on and I could hear songs, songs . . .

"See See Rider."

"At Last."

"I'll Never Smile Again" and "I'll Be Seeing You."

Aherne stares at Kay.

CHRIS'S VOICE

Next Sunday we will marry. The doorman at the theater says his minister in Harlem will marry us in his parlor. And when you finish school and the war is over we will live in France.

KAY

(Writes) My great-aunt said at my mother's funeral she saw my father hiding amid the cedar trees. She heard him singing "I Come to the Garden Alone."

That was my mother's favorite hymn.

Christopher, last Sunday we had a program at school. There was a speech on W. E. B. Du Bois who taught here . . . then music from the band.

Train cars move in darkness.

Backstage:

CHRIS

My mother said Harrison's most loved terrain is the house he was born in out there on Oglethorpe Road, that old white house with

23

the porch and columns. I think his father built that house around 1860 . . . but now he lets colored live there. Broken-down staircase, boarded-up rooms . . . should have saved that house and repaired it for us . . . it still is one of the most majestic houses in the county . . . But he lets the cousins to his colored children live there. And he finds a reason to walk on that abandoned land every day. Then he supervises the tending of the colored cemetery, his Aherne Gardens. You know that garden is in sight of his old birthplace, halfway between the house and the Flint Farms. Why would he want to do that?

I worship my father but I don't understand why he drives up the road in his Ford to the gardens.

All the colored are kin around the Aherne Farms. They are all buried there. He told me he wants to build another bower of cedar trees. I love to hear him sing "Beautiful Dreamer." When we are in church I love to hear his voice saying the Lord's Prayer.

Light on train cars moving in darkness.

Aherne stares at Kay.

He stands.

Train in darkness.

CHRIS'S VOICE
"I have finally decided," he told me.

Lights on Aherne. He speaks:

AHERNE
As you approach the entrance from the road, you see the sign in the soil, Aherne Gardens, then a winding path, a narrow path

leading back to the graves that are in a circular design beyond the weeping willow trees. And between the tombstones—roses— everything should be covered in roses.

Lights off Aherne.

CHRIS'S VOICE

He always has bags of seeds in the Ford that he has Austin, our chauffeur, leave for Reverend Douglas. He has worked on this sunup and sundown.

The train cars.

In darkness, lights beyond New York City.

KAY

(Looking out of the train window) I wonder what really happened to my mother. In the funeral parlor my great-aunt yelled at my grandmother, "You were so mean to her, so mean. Maggie said when she arrived in Cincinnati her skin was black and purple. Black and purple and crippled legs. And crying, crying."

CHRIS

(From the dressing room) Kay, I can still see my half-brothers and sister that June night on the stage of *Paris Massacre.*

My mother said, "When Harrison visits these children I have heard he often watches their piano recitals from the wings. You know he bought them a piano."

Sometimes she spoke in Latin. I asked her what she was saying. She said, "The Shade of Dido."

Before Aeneas reaches his final destination in Italy, he visits the Underworld to see the shade of his father, Anchises, who had died on the voyage from Troy to Italy.

Soon after entering the realm of the dead, Aeneas comes
to the Fields of Lamentation (lúgentés campì), the region
assigned to those who died for love. There he chances to
see Dido, the beautiful Carthaginian queen, who killed
herself after he had loved and then abandoned her.

Then:

Train cars.

*With lights from New York flooding the two cars. Kay stares from
her window.*

Harrison Aherne speaks.

It is from The Massacre at Paris*:*

> AHERNE
> How fares it with my Lord High Admiral?
> Hath he been hurt with villains in the street?
> I vow and swear as I am King of France to find and repay
> the man with death.
> With death delayed and torments never used.

Harrison Aherne reads from his book The Massacre at Paris.

> CHRIS'S VOICE
> *(From the dressing room)* Kay will never know whether her mother
> shot herself in the head or whether she was found stabbed to
> death in the freight elevator.

> AHERNE
> *(On the train, from* The Massacre at Paris*:)*

> Enter the English Agent
> Agent for England, send thy mistress word
> What this detested Jacobin hath done.

Tell her, for all this, that I hope to live,
Which if I do, the papal monarch goes
To wrack, and antichristian kingdom falls.
These bloody hands shall tear his triple crown
And fire accursed Rome about his ears.
I'll fire his crazed buildings and enforce
The papal towers to kiss the lowly earth.
Navarre, give me thy hand. I here do swear
To ruinate that wicked church of Rome
That hatcheth up such bloody practices,
And here protest eternal love to thee
And to the Queen of England specially,
Whom God hath blessed for hating papistry.

Darkness on train.

Then:

Very bright stage in New York City.

The small charming theater music, music from Bitter Sweet.

Train.

On the train Aherne stands, never taking his eyes from Kay.

Sounds of "See See Rider Blues."

Kay is staring out at the New York lights, happy.

Train dark.

Aherne stands staring at her, she has never seen him.

Still reading from his book:

A poisoned knife
Wounded and poisoned both at once

O that that damned villain were alive again
That we might torture him with some new found death.

Repeats.

Sounds of "See See Rider Blues."

———

Stage:

Darkness, then a very, very bright stage.

"See See Rider Blues."

———

Backstage:

Kay ascends the stairs to the stage.

"See See Rider Blues."

Chris goes to her. They meet.

From below, darkness a shadow . . .

They are shot dead and fall headlong down the stairs.

From somewhere, a radio, December 7, 1941:

"Today is the day that will live in infamy . . ."

Lights go bright on the wall of the storeroom.

END

Unraveling the Landscape

An Interview with Adrienne Kennedy
By Branden Jacobs-Jenkins

In December 2017, as rehearsals began for He Brought Her Heart Back in a Box *at Theatre for a New Audience, playwright Branden Jacobs-Jenkins spoke by phone with Adrienne Kennedy from her home in Virginia.*

Branden Jacobs-Jenkins: How did this play emerge?

Adrienne Kennedy: I wasn't expecting to write a play. Not in the least bit. I write loads and loads of journals, but somehow this play just emerged. Because I got angry—I was angry at my grandson's high school in Virginia. It so reminded me of Ohio State in the fifties, and that made me very angry.

What was going on with your grandson's high school?

Well, there were few Black kids, and they seemed to stand out, in an uncomfortable way that I remember. I just couldn't believe that they were going through the same thing, basically, that I went through at Ohio State. They felt very isolated.

I love stories about plays that just sort of "show up." Did this emerge out of that journaling practice, or did it arrive fully formed as a play?

The room in my son's house faces all these trees, and I'm just staring at all these trees—and I have loads of photographs. My mother kept all these photographs. I found a photograph of her boarding school, at a place called Fort Valley, Georgia. She talked about that boarding school constantly. It's very Victorian-looking. It reminded me of the Brontës. So that was a big inspiration. And I spent six summers in Georgia when I was a kid. We lived in Cleveland, but I spent six summers in Georgia, visiting my grandmother. And I've never been able to unravel that town, and all those relationships.

What amazes me is that I tend to think about the same things I've thought about all my life, and I always try to unravel those things. I just had another go at trying to unravel that town, and those six summers, and that's really what it is.

I think that all of the plays you've written since Ohio State Murders *have been wrestling very beautifully with this idea of remembrance. I especially love the kind of Gothic qualities of this new play: There are stories within stories, and images within images. Is memory a thing that you think a lot about?*

Oh, I do. I do think about the past a lot. I think about my parents a lot, because I realized how unusual they were. My father was a social worker, he was a Y secretary. My mother was a schoolteacher, she taught fifth-grade science. I think you have to get older before you realize—they put so much energy into me. And they were so concerned about me. So I think about that a lot.

Are the characters in this piece based on anyone from your life, or are they all fiction? Or are they kind of an amalgam? I hate that question, but I'm always curious. The kinds of stories that are haunting them—the stories they're telling—feel so vivid.

The stories—those are an amalgam. I don't think she would've defined herself like that, but my mother was a great storyteller. She always held me captive. She smoked Lucky Strike cigarettes, and she'd always say, "Adrienne, I wanna tell you something." She is just all over my whole writing career. And my father, because he gave speeches. Really, everything I write is a kind of mixture of his speeches and her telling me all these stories about Georgia.

It's interesting that you say you're always writing about your parents. I think every writer, probably, in some way, is doing that. Trying to unravel the mystery of your immediate origins. Do you feel close to your characters' generation?

Well, my father is born in 1904. My mother is born in 1907, and they were born right down the road from each other. They went to Morehouse, and Atlanta University, around 1930. To me, they're the greatest generation. My parents and their friends, to me, have qualities that I don't have, my children don't have. They're very imaginative, hard-working people. They created so much. My mother could teach all day, and then she could come home and cook a perfect dinner, and her house always looked perfect. They had qualities, I think, that are just so admirable.

What has the theater meant to you? What does it mean to you now?

I fell in love with the theater when I was sixteen and I saw *The Glass Menagerie*. Tennessee Williams still remains very, very important to me. Lorca is my favorite playwright, really. My husband was a grad student, and we came to New York in 1955. I love the theater of the fifties, the musicals of the fifties. I haven't been to the theater in years. And I don't consider myself a playwright, because I haven't had very many pleasant experiences when I've had my plays put on. I feel the best about scholars—the academic world. They xeroxed my plays and kept them alive. But I don't really like the theater that much, from my experiences when I've had plays put on.

I see myself as a writer. I'm a scribbler, I really am. I've been scribbling since I was six years old. I've written a lot of things that I've thrown away, I've written lots of things that will never see the light of day. Occasionally, I've had these plays up. But I owe almost everything to the academic world. Because I taught for so long, I understand that. I would always teach Amiri Baraka's *Dutchman*, I would always teach *The Seagull*. I understand the love of plays, the love of literature. That's really what I love.

Maybe the better version of the question is: What does it mean to you to write plays?

I see, I know what you're saying. I think I still owe it to *The Glass Menagerie*. Because when I saw that—we seemed to be an ideal family, but my parents had loads and loads of problems, and subsequently got a divorce. And when I saw *The Glass Menagerie* and I saw those people—even today, right this very morning, if I saw *The Glass Menagerie*, I would start weeping, weeping. It's those people, living in their living room, with all their problems. That inspired me so much. *Death of a Salesman* also. I might owe something to my Ohio State drama teacher, who gave me an A— the only A I ever got at Ohio State, practically. Because she said, "You really understand plays." So I was reaching for what people had said. All through my twenties, I wrote constantly. I went to the New School, I went to the American Theater Wing. When I went on a trip to Africa, we were out of the country thirteen months, and that's when I wrote *Funnyhouse of a Negro*. And the monologues that I had written in Ghana, and the monologues that I wrote in Rome—I realized that they had something. It was the landscape: the landscape of Ghana, the landscape of West Africa, and the landscape of Rome.

What is it about a landscape that speaks to you in that way? That feels very Brontë-esque too. Their whole thing was the moors, the moors, the moors . . .

I think I'm still trying to imitate that! I really do. I've been to several writers' houses. I've been to O'Neill's house, and to the Brontë cottage. I ran upon the heather. I mean, I was old, I was in my sixties!

I do want to say, of course—and I'm sure it's true with you—I love pen and paper. The typewriter. I love writers. I'm very in awe of writers. That has never gone away. And I like pop culture—music, pop songs. I'm a kid of the radio, you know? And I still have my radio.

I love that. You don't happen to watch Netflix, do you?

I do watch Netflix.

There's something similar to Netflix that I watch, which has just tons and tons of old movies. I think about you often when I'm watching it, because A Movie Star Has to Star in Black and White is one of my favorite plays. It's this incredible repository. Right now I'm watching Laura, by Otto Preminger.

I've seen all those movies a hundred times. Those people—Bette Davis, Hitchcock, all those people—I probably will always underestimate what I've learned from them.

Even in this new play—there's a kind of thriller aspect to it, right? There's this simmering dread throughout the whole thing, that does kind of remind me a bit of Hitchcock.

Hitchcock is very important to me. *Vertigo*, of course, is my favorite. I learned so much from those movies. As a kid growing up in a place like Cleveland, we did go to the movies every Saturday. It was five cents, and it was something that the white kids—the Italian kids—did with the Black kids. That was the only thing we ever really did together. We went to see the movies for five cents, and of course, it was a double feature.

The place where the two characters in your play meet is the movie theater, right? He says, "I saw you at Bitter Sweet." *I love that.*

That's a real place. The movie theater in Montezuma, which is the real name of that town, was so dramatic. It was this tiny movie theater, with a whites-only section of regular movie seats. My grandmother would only take me once, because she despised it so. The Blacks had to walk up the back stairwell, and there were four or five benches where Blacks sat. That movie theater was so important. The only one in the town, of course.

I went there from 1936 to 1943, something like that. I have a photograph of that movie theater. But all those movies—Bette Davis movies are very important to me. Because Bette Davis was a person who had violent feelings. And everybody said I was such a sweet little kid, clinging to my mother's dress. But I couldn't understand why I felt like I did, and Bette Davis was a release of all these violent feelings that were going on inside me.

Pop culture becomes the way out for so many people, the space where you can imagine something other than your life. Which is the first step to changing it, I guess.

I like that. A way out. That's exactly what it was.

Is there anything else you want to talk about—about the play or anything—before we end? It's very haunting. I've been thinking about it since I read it, kind of nonstop.

I think the play is, to me, a victory. Because it is, on paper, things that I can't stop thinking about.

BRANDEN JACOBS-JENKINS is a Brooklyn-based writer and award-winning theater artist. His plays include *Girls, Everybody, War, Gloria, Appropriate, Neighbors,* and *An Octoroon.* He teaches at The University of Texas at Austin.

A version of this interview originally appeared in an issue of Theatre for a New Audience's *360° Viewfinder* for the play's world premiere in 2017. This version was then printed in the September 2019 issue of *American Theatre* magazine alongside the publication of *He Brought Her Heart Back in a Box.* Reprinted with permission from Theatre for a New Audience, Branden Jacobs-Jenkins, and *American Theatre* magazine.

Etta and Ella
on the Upper West Side

Place

There are scenes of the Hudson River.
And scenes of 89th Street.

The Narrative

A woman's voice that turns out to be Ella's voice.
Ella whom Etta strangled in the tunnel near the New Haven railway station.

Her voice is always the narrator. We don't realize it is her voice until she appears to her sister late one night in Etta's room on 89th Street.

They are almost twins in torn, old evening gowns.

Etta's voice on answering machine: "Harold. Harold. Etta Harrison calling. Harold."

Her voice is desperate.

Not only did she teach and write, she sometimes acted in her own plays.

Her desperate voice is dramatic:

"I. Can. See your light.
"I want to talk to you about a coming murder, Harold."

1

Troupe was unable to stop Etta Harrison from leaving messages on his office machine about a coming murder. In July when he went into the office of his brownstone sometimes there were as many as five messages from her in one night.

89th Street, 32S.
Rooms facing the street.
Crates of unpacked books.
Alcove piano.
Table of books.
He is renovating other floors.
Floor-through/alley can be seen.
He always practices same *Polonaise*, Chopin.
He sits, writes.
His books are on Black music *[Ellen Southern, Amiri Baraka]*.

He is compiling a gigantic anthology of Negro Spirituals, and sings snatches of songs.

Unpacked crates of books everywhere.

[Sometimes he walks to the roof of the brownstone and looks to the Hudson.]

Beyond his table: alcove piano, single bed, piles of books, more crates.

Answering machine on the table where Troupe works. Etta's voice: "Harold! Harold!" He does not reply.

2

Harold Troupe: Black, forty, portly, always dressed in suit, vest, shirt, tie. Handsome, melancholy, professor at City College. He is compiling an anthology on Negro Spirituals.

[He orders bacon cheeseburgers.

Practices piano.

Writes from piles of notes.]

3

Etta lives across the street on 89th Street.

In a brownstone.

In a room that faces a garden and a plane tree.

It is a hot New York night.

Her room: books, china, vases of flowers, floral design. On table papers.

She is always working on stories.

Winters she teaches.

Troupe can see the doorway on 89th Street of her brownstone.

And a side window of her brownstone.

She lives on the third floor.

4

He had forgotten about Etta and Ella Harrison in recent years.
They weren't prominent anymore in his circle.
Since the strangling incident and their public fights.

He had been surprised to see that Etta was a member of the Vanishing Literary Club, until he learned she was an old friend of Jerry Loren's and he was making an opera of some of her early writing.

When Troupe had seen Etta on Broadway at the bookstore she'd looked hopeless and her dress careless.

(At Shakespeare & Co. on Broadway.)

Etta wears a wrinkled, old evening gown. Hair upswept, sneakers.

She is looking at books on shelves on the sidewalk.

When she sees Troupe, she turns and runs toward 79th Street.

Etta: Forty, once beautiful, small, pale, dark hair she wears in an upsweep, huge eyes resemble the beautiful actress Ellen Holly.

5

NARRATIVE

Nothing like the dazzling suits she and her sister used to wear to MLA meetings. He remembered especially one Christmas in New York their dress—their suits, the coats and shoes—had been talked about constantly in the elevator of the Sheraton. He remembered them coming down to breakfast together, hair in upsweeps, pearls, high heels, laughing together. Everyone wanted to join them on their excursions, their teas at the Waldorf.

But he did also remember now, after Ella had given a paper on the history of their childhood neighborhood in Ohio, in the elevator she had burst into tears and said:

"My paper didn't have half the impact it should have. In her presentation my sister used parts of an interview I showed her. But

I'm the one who spent the winter in Cleveland talking to all those people."

And then she laughed.

6, 7, 8

NARRATIVE
Troupe was surprised to see in an interview the next day in the *Amsterdam News* that they were both planning separate books on their brother, who had been mute the last years of his life because of an automobile accident. And they *each* had the idea of holding imaginary conversations with him.

One morning Troupe sent his researcher Robert to the library to find an old *Black Scholar* magazine.

"It should be about 1990 Winter," he said. "There was an article Ella wrote about Etta. I want to read it."

[Robert: Small, European, scholar.]

9, 10

Troupe reads aloud of *Black Scholar*. The interview is preceded by a short bio of Ella.

"Nine years ago Ella Harrison married the well-known writer Henderson Young. Ella Harrison is currently a fellow at the Bunting Institute in Cambridge, Massachusetts. She is writing about her family which includes a study of the South in the twenties, the Depression, and World War II.

"Following is an interview between Harrison and equally well-known sister Etta. Etta Harrison is currently teaching in New Haven. She's traveled extensively in Africa with her ex-husband— Fanon's biographer."

[Troupe walks around a crate-filled room, reading.
One crate: china from his family.]

NARRATIVE

Troupe reads.

Scene:

Etta/Ella. *[They look alike.]*

Ella: Etta what are you teaching this semester?

Etta: Creative writing and my play. I have pieces I wrote in Ghana on the savannas and drives in Liberia through the Goodrich plantation. These pieces were experiments with narrative.

Ella: During the first days in Liberia you used narrative from your first novels, *People* and *Strange Possessions*. At least that's what you told me. Why is it you don't write or talk about the murder of your baby daughters by the English professor who was their father.

Etta: He's free. Somehow he's free.

Ella: But you know he killed himself that night in 1952.

(Suddenly Etta stood up.)

Etta: Ella I've asked my editor, can I stop you from writing articles about me? He told me to leave you alone. I told him
you're making me sick. "I think if you leave her alone she'll
stop. I don't want to further upset you, Etta. But I saw parts
of a manuscript she submitted to Grove on you. Do you want
to see it? I took a look at it to see if she's violating your legal
rights. I feel this is leading to something terrible between
you." And it is.

(Etta left the interview.)

12

He laughs.

Practices Chopin.

Sometimes Etta'd think about how her sister had copied her upsweep hairstyle. Even now as an apparition, Ella's hair was carefully arranged in the hairstyle Etta was known for.

Troupe sings.

13

Troupe called Etta one afternoon in June. He had never called her. He started talking about the late seventies when he had to hire people to take care of Kay and Boulting after their mother died. He'd promised their mother he'd look out for them. And now they wanted to get away from him. They hadn't even wanted him to come to the Vanishing. And he hung up. Kay and Boulting were the children of an English woman Troupe had lived with.

For some reason, Etta thought of what the Vanishing had read the night before:

Troupe looks out his front window down to Etta's door almost directly across 89th Street.

Etta, in her room, thinking of the Vanishing meeting on Central Park West.

Members: Troupe; Kay; Boulting; Jerry Loren, songwriter.
His parlor, herself.
She remembers them sitting.

14

Robert/Troupe.

Troupe was determined to discover more what led to Ella's strangling.

He sent Robert once more to the 42nd Street Library. Robert brought back another *Black Scholar* with a longer piece by Ella, a longer version of the 1992 piece. He remembered Ella had written a play about her sister's devastating college years and her play had received considerable attention in the Ohio Press and she'd sold it to television. The Press ignored Etta's version of her own life (which had been performed earlier at the same theater) and considered it an inferior piece. This happened the spring before Yale. It was no doubt Ella cherished and coveted her sister's college tragedy.

At the end was a story Ella wrote when she was twenty.

Sitting in his crate-filled room Troupe laughed again.

Troupe had never realized how much the sisters had written together. And how in their separate stories they had used the same names for their characters. And fought over the name Suzanne. And over the years it was impossible to distinguish their experiences.

No wonder, he thought, their minds were in such turmoil. This jealousy, he now heard from Robert, extended into every phase of their lives.

In their collected work each claimed material from their Ohio childhood, Ohio State, their years in New York, their trips to Africa.

Robert said I heard they first stopped speaking to each other over stories of their relatives and both claimed an early story about their cousin. Finally they both signed it. And from what he'd heard Robert said he doubted seriously that Ella was living peacefully in the Oakland.

15

NARRATIVE

Robert/Troupe.

Etta/Ella.

Hills. From what he'd heard of her she probably had a new plan and would certainly retaliate from the musical Etta and Jerry Loren were working on about their family.

"I remember seeing the sisters once walking in the eucalyptus trees at Berkeley. They had on pink dresses and held hands," Robert said.

"I didn't know they both loved the same people, their cousins, the photographs of their grandparents, their parents. I didn't know that even then there was a dispute over the division of the family scrapbooks."

Robert said they'd gotten into a bad argument at NYU at a public lecture in the Tisch School of the Arts on stage.

Ella contended that Etta had never paid any attention whatsoever to their cousin, and laughed when she heard he ran away. And she'd laughed when she saw him with Sylvia Klein.

"There was no such person as Sylvia Klein," Etta said tensely right in front of the writing students, "we made her up." And she kept laughing tensely. Then they couldn't agree on what sections of the story to read aloud.

For the first time Troupe felt he understood their violent pre-occupations. He knew they had been superb teachers but he saw how he'd never understood how unstable they were under their upsweep hairdos and corsages on 1940s black dresses.

16

Scenes:

The Vanishing Literary Club.

Walking.

One Sunday the Vanishing watched *Breakfast at Tiffany's* and went for a walk across the Brooklyn Bridge. At Brooklyn Academy of Music they saw a play by Wole Soyinka called *The Swamp Dwellers*.

In her room facing the garden, Etta on the phone.

[Etta phoning the precinct.]

She told them she wanted them to know there would be a coming murder. And while she had them on the phone she wondered did they know what happened to the Thalia and the New Yorker (her favorite movie theaters on the Upper West Side). Why had they torn them down? And had anyone claimed responsibility for the bombing at 72nd and Broadway?

(She gets their answering machine.)

17

Troupe. Rooms.

All summer Troupe worked on an essay on Professor Thomas Dorsey. Although Dorsey and "Precious Lord, Take My Hand" were subjects he'd written about thirty years ago, he'd promised a young filmmaker he'd narrate a new essay about Dorsey and the lyrics to "Precious Lord."

> Precious Lord, take my hand,
> Lead me on, let me stand.
> I am tired. I am weak. I am worn
> Through the storm, through the night,
> Lead me on to the light.
> Take my hand, precious Lord,
> Lead me home.

> *(When he is singing it is emotional.)*

18, 19

Troupe thought of Etta and Ella.

Etta dreamed she saw Harold Troupe upon the shores of a noon-day sea in a dark mood, a jealous mood.

Etta in her room realized she had made a mistake in confiding in Troupe. She remembered all the scathing articles he'd written about his contemporaries. And the lawsuits he'd been involved in. She so hoped when her eyes improved that she could make a comeback . . . a high academic post. Perhaps a presidency. It would be a mistake to seek Troupe's help. Still, she went on help-lessly leaving him messages.

Scenes:

When the Vanishing met, Troupe insisted on showing Etta a small bedroom she could have most of the winter. He would be on a lecture tour. Etta went upstairs and opened a door. She found herself within a tiny bedroom. She felt a daybed, a desk. She knew Troupe had never totally renovated the second and third floors. There were alcoves behind walls, stairwells that led to rooms behind the old kitchen, and a sealed-up dining room. An entire back staircase still existed. When Etta opened another door she was in a closet where this staircase began.

"Does Troupe hope to trap me here?" she thought. "And why?"

That night she dreamed she asked her old student from Prague if she could see Etta's fate. "The night is the sole time we can decipher the decrees of fate," the student said.

The next day Robert, Troupe's researcher, called Etta. He said, "Professor Troupe's concerned about your confusion, your eyes. He was upset you got lost on the closed stairwell last night. He again wants you to know you're welcome to stay here this winter."

Etta wrote that night:

Am I going to be murdered in Troupe's stairwell?

The Vanishing met at the Carousel in Central Park.

20

NARRATIVE

Ella/Etta.

On August 2nd Ella's apparition visited Etta. She carried a single lamp and sat beside her bed. Its rays fell over Etta's face.

Ella was happy to see how her sister's countenance had changed over the summer. Her color was gone, the lips pallid, fierce was her struggle between reason and madness.

Ella sat quietly, Etta unconscious of her presence.

After a pause Ella spoke.

Etta sprang up—the apparition of her foe.

"Am I dreaming?"

"No, you are awake. You tried to kill me.

"I confess to having hurt you. I could not help myself when I tried to strangle you under the underpass in New Haven. You had no right to take my life and make a play."

Scene:

A deserted wing of Yeshiva School faced Riverside Drive where abandoned children hid. Shattered steps led to a yard of stones and weeds. Etta sat on the steps and wrote:

Someone will be murdered.

21

Boulting: Polepunt, curly brown hair, small.

Kay, his sister—they look alike

I think I know who the murdered will be.

Scenes:

That Sunday she tried to follow one of the members of the Vanishing to warn him. She stood on the other side of the street opposite the Strand Bookstore and watched Boulting come out. She started to cross the street but her eyes hurt violently. She went home on the Number 5 bus. "Why," she thought, "do I follow Boulting? My only friend."

Sometimes in the night Etta walked up the closed stairwell that led to the walled-up original dining room of the brownstone. The floor of the stairs was covered with sand from sand-blasting on the street years ago. She thought she heard a prolonged laugh. But by now she knew it was her sister's apparition. She tried to look through a slit in the door into the vanished dining room but she could see nothing. When Etta came back into her room there was a key on the floor underneath the lamp. She picked it up.

And decided to try it everywhere she went in Troupe's house. She discovered finally the key was to the tiny shed at the end of the garden. The shed had several sets of garden implements, shining. They looked unused.

Boulting told Kay that he'd heard from their cousin, who lived near Elizabeth in London and had seen her on the King's Road, that Elizabeth was planning to seek legal custody of their daughter Rose.

That night Kay dreamed James and his daughter Rose were sailing on a fatal river.

He called back to her: "Let us sit down, my sister. I am wearied with the heat of the sun." They sat beneath a plane tree, an arbutus clustering around them. James read Kay a song, "Regrets for Childhood":

It is not that our earlier Heaven
Escapes its April showers,
Or that to childhood's heart is given
No snake amidst the flowers.
Ah! Twined with grief
Each brightest leaf,
That's wreath'd us by the Hours!

Young though we be, the Past may sting,
The Present feed its sorrow;
But hope shines bright on every thing
That waits us with the morrow.
Like sunlit glades,
The dimmest shades
Some rosy beam can borrow.

When Boulting came to see Kay the next day he asked her to walk with him to Columbus Avenue to buy some paper dolls of Victorian royalty that he'd seen for Rose.

Kay suggested they stop at Chemical Bank. She wanted to give James money. He wouldn't take it.

"That's our mother's money," he said. "I'm going to get money of my own."

As they walked down Columbus Avenue, James told Kay about a story he was writing:

It's about a severed head.

Boulting and his sister Kay.

22

NARRATIVE
"My poor brother," Kay thought.

She again tried to get him to move in with her. His building was broken into every day.

Even though she was exhausted, Etta read Boulting's Zen poems and tried to help him organize his tapes of the "Sounds of Streams." He was the only member of the Vanishing that she let into her humid book-filled rooms. He was concerned about the noise of the sand-blasting in the street and the sand-filled air. He brought her a potassium drink and stargazers.

"You can stay with me, Etta, until the sand-blasting on the next apartment is over," he said. "I can clear out a room I have, now that Elizabeth and Rose are gone."

68

He took her to the Village in a taxi. He said he wanted her to see one of his favorite movies, the 1960s *Ipcress File*. Afterwards James insisted on going to East 2nd Street and showing Etta the room of dolls, a baby carriage, a cradle, flowered wallpaper, miniature Dover books he'd read to his daughter Rose. It was the only decorated room in the apartment.

He took Etta back home. But before he left, he read to her from a book on Beethoven he'd had since college. Boulting was the only person Etta had shown her pages of *She Talks to Beethoven* to.

"I hope I finish by autumn," she said, "and by Christmas I hope to have it performed somewhere."

"I'll get someone to put it on for you," he said. "I'll be Beethoven."

Boulting and Etta.

23

Ella/Etta.

On the night of the murder she possessed a knife.

On the night Ella's apparition led Etta to the Drive in the moon-light a water main broke in the street. They passed rows of torches and barricades. It was just as the Vanishing had read their very first night:

"By the light of these torches, parties of fugitives from previous bombings encountered each other, some hurrying toward the sea, others fleeing the sea back to the land, for the ocean had retreated from the shore."

It seemed to Etta that utter darkness suddenly lay over the street.

"I can't go any further," she said to Ella. But Ella held her arm. Then they passed firemen bearing more torches heading toward the burst water mains.

But Ella forced her down a remote stone staircase toward the Hudson shore. Etta couldn't escape.

On that murder night Etta's eyes hurt violently, but against her will her sister had pulled her out of Troupe's brownstone and along Riverside Drive, all the way to 79th Street. And down to the gully: the apparition consumed Etta. Ella's apparition fell into the grass, when Etta tried to stab her . . .

"There's someone here recording the sounds of the Hudson," Ella laughed.

"Someone you must see."

Ella's apparition had led her to Boulting. Etta kept stabbing. Her only friend.

24

Hear Troupe singing.

Etta's voice on the answering machine:

"Is this the precinct?
While I have you on the phone.
Why did you tear down the New Yorker?"

END

Mom, How Did You Meet The Beatles?

———

*A True Story of London
in the 1960s*

*By Adrienne Kennedy and
Adam P. Kennedy*

PRODUCTION HISTORY

Mom, How Did You Meet The Beatles? had its world premiere at
The Public Theater (Oskar Eustis, Artistic Director; Mara Manus,
Executive Director) in New York, on February 12, 2008. It was
directed by Peter DuBois. The scenic and costume design were by
Alexander Dodge, the lighting design was by Michael Chybowski,
the sound design was by Walter Trarbach; the production stage
manager was Elizabeth Miller. The cast was:

ADRIENNE KENNEDY   Brenda Pressley
ADAM KENNEDY   William DeMerrit

Characters

ADRIENNE KENNEDY: The Adrienne character is often hesitant, emotional, joyous, and sad. The conversation with her son is the *first time* she has spoken about her time in London during the 1960s.

ADAM KENNEDY: Throughout the play, the Adam character is curious as to events he's heard something about. This is the *first time* he's heard the story from his mother.

Authors' Notes

In London, in the 1960s, there was music everywhere. The Beatles, The Stones, The Supremes, James Brown, Aretha, Jimi Hendrix, music from the musical *Hair*, Dylan, etc.

Specific 1960s songs were used in The Public Theater production. We have indicated who the artists were so that the music can approximate these sounds.

Also regarding The Public Theater production: We used specific London scenes—pictures of the National Theatre, Primrose Hill, Maida Vale, Adrienne and Adam on Chalcot Crescent, and the Royal Court.

Adrienne Kennedy enters center stage and remains there. Adam Kennedy is seated close to the wings, partially seen.

Adrienne wears a pretty dress—silver was popular—and perhaps ballerina shoes. Adam wears dark trousers and a white shirt.

Throughout the play, Adrienne looks at the audience. There are only a few moments when she glances back at the actor behind her.

Behind Adrienne are scenes of London during the 1960s.

ADAM KENNEDY

How did you come to work with The Beatles?

ADRIENNE KENNEDY

Joe [*Joseph C. Kennedy*] and I were separated and somehow you and I ended up living on Bedford Street for about eight months and I was miserable. I didn't see a way out. Gillian Walker came to see a production of *The Owl Answers* at the Theatre de Lys. She was a New York career girl with all this energy and enthusiasm and this love for *Funnyhouse of a Negro*. She had already seen *Funnyhouse*. She told me she worked for Ted Mann's theater Circle in the Square. She was Ted's assistant, but she was far more. She really was co-producer. I knew Ted Mann because I had studied at Circle in the Square . . . *Funnyhouse* . . . that's where *Funnyhouse* had its very first workshop production at Circle in the Square on Bleecker Street.

She said, "Maybe we could commission you to write a play." Bedford Street was only a stone's throw from Bleecker Street. So I walked around there. You were in school in kindergarten. I walked around there and went up to see Ted. He said I'd like to commission you to write a play. So . . . that just sounded so good to me. He said, "What do you want to write?" Well, a couple of years before, Joedy had given me a book about The Beatles . . . John Lennon's nonsense book. I was always crazy about this book. It's a little blue book. It has a photograph of John Lennon on the cover and these little nonsense verses. I was always just so taken with it. So I said I'd like to make a play of John Lennon's nonsense writings. I thought that really sounded great . . . maybe go to London and meet The Beatles or something. *(Laughs)* It was crazy in a way, because I was in my mid-thirties. But . . . you know . . . that's what I said.

He said, "Well I know John Lennon's publisher. His name is Tom Maschler. I'll write to Tom Maschler and ask him . . . you know . . . maybe you could get permission to make a play out of John Lennon's nonsense book." He didn't say that's crazy or whatever. So Gillian wrote the letter, "A great idea," she said.

She wrote to Tom Maschler in London, and Maschler I think answered right away . . . and he said something like, "Tell her if she's ever in London to look me up." He said something like, "That sounds interesting. I can't make any promises, but tell her if she's ever in London to look me up."

Well I was a desperate person *(Laughing)* . . . you know what I mean. And I thought I was going to get a Guggenheim. I was almost sure I was going to get a Guggenheim. And I'm stuck on Bedford Street. And there we were and I didn't know what I was going to do. So I said what I'll do, since I'm going to get a Guggenheim, I already had a Rockefeller Grant and, of course, Joe was giving me alimony . . . so, I'll take my little money and I'll go to London.

And . . . it was just a desperate move, a totally desperate move. I was walking down the street, on a Tuesday. We went to London on Thursday. And on Tuesday, I was walking down Bleecker Street . . . Gillian said we could spend the last night in her house at the Dakota, which turned out to be very strange, because that's where John Lennon was murdered.

I was walking down Bleecker Street and I saw Diana Sands. Diana Sands always regretted that by the time *Funnyhouse* reached Off-Broadway she couldn't be in it. She was on Broadway in *The Owl and the Pussycat* with Alan Alda. Diana was the original Sarah in *Funnyhouse*. She said, "Adrienne, I've always felt so terrible about it . . . Where are you going?" She was going to Circle in the Square too. She had an appointment with Ted Mann.

As we walked I told her I was going to London in a few days. She said, "I've just come back from London and I want to give you a list of people you can look up there." She'd been doing *The Owl and the Pussycat* in the West End.

She said, "Where will you be the last night here?" The . . . last night . . . was a Wednesday. I told her the Dakota at Gillian's. She came to the Dakota and brought a long list of all these people. I remember she told me to call Ricki Huston first because she had a child your age. So I had all these people in the theater to look up.

With that list and this message from Tom Maschler—on the strength of that I pulled myself together and took us to London in search . . . of . . . something.

We stayed at the Dakota the last night. I've always thought that that was very strange. The Dakota, I don't know if you remember . . . the Dakota had some rooms . . . rooms up on the top floor that servants used to sleep in . . . babysitters and housekeepers. Some tenants had a room like that. Gillian's friends used to stay in that little room. They were enchanting little rooms. We stayed in that little room upstairs for our last night.

And then we set off . . . we left in the morning for London. And I remember being at JFK. It was November . . . something like November 27, 1966. It was November 26 or November 27. And you were so trusting. You were just . . . you know . . . I said, "Adam, we're going to London." And you were always just so trusting. And we're at the airport and I'm talking to you about going to London. And we got on a plane and went to London. We . . . I think had about four hundred dollars maybe five but no more. I didn't know. I just wanted to change my life.

Gillian had given me the name of what they called a "bed-sit." They didn't call them pensiones; they called them bed-sitters. A writer she knew lived in one in Earls Court. She told me to go there and ask for him. It would be a place to stay.

London theme music begins playing.

We arrived in London at about ten o'clock at night. And I went to this bed-sit and I asked for this writer. A woman said he wasn't there. And she was hostile . . . the woman who ran it. You could tell she was shocked that I was Black and that I was asking to stay in this bed-sit. I said, "Well, doesn't this writer live here?" She said, "He's not here. He's in Paris." Or something like that. "You can't stay here."

Gillian had another name written down . . . the Basil Street Hotel. I didn't know the Basil Street Hotel is one of the fanciest little hotels in London. So it's ten o'clock at night. We're trudging with our suitcases looking for a taxi.

London theme music begins to fade.

I don't know a soul in London. All I have is addresses, Diana Sands' theater connections. So we go to the Basil Street Hotel at about eleven at night. And they were so nice. This beautiful little hotel. It's right around the corner from Harrods.

I'm sure by now it costs a fortune. And it had these enchanting little rooms with wallpaper . . .

Tea dance music begins playing.

. . . like an Agatha Christie novel . . . Colonel so and so came down for breakfast. They gave tea dances. We were only there about two weeks, but they gave tea dances in the afternoon and Colonel so and so is dancing with his wife. And they were so nice to us. I think they were nice to us because . . . *(Pause)* . . . you didn't see many American Blacks in London. And I think people were just a little taken aback. I really do.

Tea dance music begins to fade.

I think I had the letter from Tom Maschler, but I'm not sure. But I certainly had his address, Bedford Square and the name of the publisher, Jonathan Cape. And I had Ricki Huston's address. The very next day I called Tom Maschler and I called Ricki Huston.

Ricki's theme music should be in the realm of Jagger, Hendrix, Aretha, The Supremes.

I had seen Ricki's picture many times . . . on the cover of *Life* magazine . . . in magazines skiing with John Huston . . . at home with John Huston. She answered the phone. I couldn't believe I was talking to her. She said, "Darling, I give teas on Sunday. You're a friend of Diana's. Please come by. Come by on Sunday."

I called Tom Maschler. He said he couldn't see me until that next week. We went to Ricki's on Sunday. The Hustons lived in Maida Vale No. 31 on the canal . . . Little Venice. The rooms were palatial and filled with art objects. She was very beautiful . . . with three beautiful children . . . Tony, Anjelica, Allegra. A governess lived with them. They seemed to like us. And they particularly liked you. I don't want to underestimate that. People were taken with you. I had you dressed up in this little blazer and shirt. It was very expensive. Not that it cost as much as Prince Charles . . . but it was expensive. When Joedy came from Sierra Leone they liked him too. Ricki put his picture on her dresser. So Ricki sort of took us on as her American friends . . . her Sundays at four.

Ricki's music begins to fade.

By the next Tuesday . . . I think it was the next Tuesday . . . I took you . . . Tom Maschler said he couldn't see me until like 5:00 P.M. He said, "I'll see you at the end of the day." He said, "I want to tell you . . . I can't promise you anything except that you can come by." I said, "You told me, if ever I was in London, I could look you up." *(Laughs)* He never dreamed that I was flying to London then. It was just a little crazy.

So we went . . . I came up from the Underground. His office was on the right, Bedford Square. We went in and I left you sitting in the little lobby. It was dark. It's December now . . . a week later *[after leaving New York]*. It's the first week in December and it's dark and cold. I went into his office. He turned out to be a young man about . . . twenty-eight . . . dark-haired, intense.

He said, "What are you doing here in London?" I said, "I have a Rockefeller Grant and I'm probably going to get a Guggenheim and I'm just here for a little while." I told everyone that, I was just there for a couple of weeks. I told everybody that, because I really didn't know. I had already sent him twenty pages. I don't know when I did that. I think I did that from New York. I just sat down real quick and sent him twenty pages of *The Lennon Play*.

He said, "I can't give you money and I can't give you the rights to make a play out of John Lennon's *In His Own Write*. But what I will do, I will tell John. I will tell John about you." He said, "That's all I can promise you." He said, "But you will have to finish the whole thing, and I can't pay you." He said it was nice meeting me. So we left.

Tea dance music begins playing.

So we were there at the Basil Street Hotel. We went to Ricki's the next Sunday and that gave me a sense of security. Ricki was like that. She either embraced you or I guess she didn't pay any attention to you. But she embraced us.

. . . I remember that Christmas we went to the pantomime *Cinderella* at The Palladium. Do you remember that? . . .

Tea dance music out.

We were still at the Basil Street Hotel. Then . . . an American couple, Ann and Carlton Colcord, had produced *A Rat's Mass* in Rome. I had corresponded with them. They knew what I looked like from a photo I had sent them. They had lived in South America and now lived in Rome.

ADAM

And you had never met them?

ADRIENNE

I had never met them. We were standing on the corner facing Harrods . . . all these kinds of . . . I don't know . . . these weird occurrences. We were standing on the corner facing Harrods, starting to cross the street and go to the Basil Street Hotel, and this man was standing next to me. He said, "Aren't you Adrienne Kennedy?" And I said, "Why, yes." And he said, "Well, I'm Carlton Colcord."

London theme music begins. It should be in the vein of The Byrds, music of the era.

He said he too was staying at the Basil Street. He said, "Ann and I are thinking of moving to London. Ann's coming here in a few days, and she's going to stay at the Basil Street Hotel. We have two little children. In fact, we have a little boy who's Adam's age."

It had always been on my mind that we should go back to New York, and I began to feel like we couldn't stay at the Basil Street Hotel. I began to feel like maybe we should go back to New York. But I'd given up that little horrible apartment on Bedford Street. So I couldn't go back. The apartment we lived in before Joe and I separated, 400 Central Park West had been so beautiful.

We had Ricki's teas and everybody was nice to us.

Then we stayed at a bed-sitter on Queen's Gate Terrace. You walked out, and there at the corner was Kensington Palace. I was excited . . . then Janet Miguell, Ricki's friend, who helped run the Leslie Waddington Art Gallery said, "You and Adam can stay with us for a while."

She lived in an apartment across from Olympia. We saw a boat show there once. The apartment was a kind of building I'd never seen . . . gigantic, red structure with large, wandering apartments. Janet and Gina *[Ricki's best friend]* lived there. Gina was a painter who later married an Olympic athlete. Large paintings were on the walls.

I kept working on the Lennon pages, and working on the pages and working on the pages. Then I forgot about it. I said, "Maybe I should go back home." I called up the Guggenheim. I said, "I know you don't announce the Guggenheim until April 1st" . . . and this was January . . . "but do you think I'm going to get a Guggenheim?" A secretary said she did not generally give out that kind of information. But she said she would talk to the Foundation and find out. *(Laughs)* I don't know why I did these kinds of things. Here I am in London *[in January]* and I need to know whether I'm going to get the Guggenheim in April. *(More laughter)* I don't know where I got that from. My mother would die. I mean I don't know where I got the nerve to do things like that.

Someone called me. "You are going to get a Guggenheim."

ADAM

So how much was that worth? How much was the Guggenheim?

ADRIENNE

It was eight thousand, five hundred dollars, which was a fortune back then. People lived on eight thousand, five hundred dollars.

I knew it was enough money for us to live on for a year. Joe was giving me money each month. I had a Rockefeller Grant. Rockefeller Grants were three thousand, five hundred dollars. But I had spent quite a bit of the Rockefeller Grant already.

We were just lucky. Now I felt we could stay in London. So I went out looking for apartments. You know there was this big racial thing in London. And there weren't many American Blacks . . . when I showed up people seemed a little . . .

ADAM

When you say there was a "big racial thing," what do you mean?

ADRIENNE

People were very aware that you were not white. At that time a lot of West Indians were moving to London. You know there was a tradition of Africans living and going to school in England: Cambridge, Oxford, and University of London. But now the British thought too many West Indians were moving to London. It was very much in the air.

People would be surprised that I was Black. I would call first after seeing an apartment in the *London Times*. I didn't know what I was doing.

Primrose Hill music begins. It is joyous.

So Janet Miguell said, "Adrienne, I don't think you know how to find an apartment in London. I'll find you an apartment." She made a few phone calls. Then she said, "You should live up in Primrose Hill. A lot of Americans live up there. It's not expensive but it's beautiful. Some writers live there but it's still working class."

So I went up there in a taxi. It seemed far away. We went up this street; I think it's called Albert Road. There was the zoo and Primrose Hill. Janet told me Karl Marx once walked there and Sylvia Path had lived on Chalcot Square. She had found an apartment for us. She said, "They're thrilled. I told them you're a Guggenheim Fellow. They have a pretty little apartment at the top of their house." I remember it was seventy pounds a month, which was about two hundred and ten dollars.

So we went there. They said you're a writer and a Guggenheim Fellow. They let us move in right away. It was on the corner, 39 Chalcot Crescent. You went up the stairs to the top floor of their house. It was a beautiful little living room, hallway, kitchen, and a bedroom that faced a garden.

The day we moved to Primrose Hill I got a phone call: "Hello Adrienne, this is James Earl Jones." We had met when Ellen Holly had introduced us backstage at a production of *Macbeth* that Joe Papp had done in Washington Square Park. I remembered his unusually intense brown eyes. "I'm in London and I don't know anyone."

My new friends all wanted to meet him. Ricki invited a group to her house. Jimmy was preparing to do a movie in France with the Burtons, a Graham Greene novel. His mention of the Burtons reminded me of my obsession with Elizabeth Taylor. "Jimmy, when you're making the movie with the Burtons, could you get me Elizabeth Taylor's autograph?" "I will," he said matter-of-factly. He came to London several times while filming the movie, once bringing with him a man who was writing a book on Africa. Finally at the end of the summer Jimmy came to London again. Would he be going back to France?

"The filming is over," he said. "Did you ever get Elizabeth Taylor's autograph?"

"No. I wanted to because I knew you really wanted it, but I felt funny asking her for an autograph."

Primrose Hill music begins to fade.

The man Jimmy had brought to visit was Alex Haley. He came up the stairs full of energy, carrying books under his arm. He sat on a gray silk couch and we talked about young marriages, which we both had experienced. He told me that he was writing a book that would trace his ancestors back to West Africa. Although I had been to West Africa with Joe for six months and knew it had changed my entire consciousness, I still laughed. The idea of a person tracing his family back that far was funny to me. "You shouldn't laugh," he said very genially, "in fact you should trace yours." I never forgot it.

After we'd been there for about four months, the family decided they didn't like having visitors in their house. It wasn't renovated. And when we went up the stairwell we passed by their upstairs rooms.

It was near July, the landlord said, "Mrs. Kennedy, there's a man down the street and he's stationed in Nigeria. They have two floors and they're for rent. It's only five pounds more than this and it's all furnished." And I'll never forget. I went down there and looked at it. "I called the agent for you and I told him you're an American, you're over here on a Guggenheim and he said he'll lease it to you for a year." So we took our suitcases and went to No. 35. And to me it was like Shangri-la. It was a beautiful two floors of a house with a garden, two baths, beautiful bedrooms. It was furnished very traditionally. There was a living room that faced the garden.

The dining room had a mantel piece, striped wallpaper and a big dark dining table with chairs. And the living room had a settee. It wasn't a couch, it was a settee. And striped gold wallpaper. Then you walked down three steps and there was a kitchen. It faced the garden. And you walked down about five or six more steps and there were two bedrooms, with two baths. Your room faced the garden. To me, it was like heaven.

I never heard from Tom Maschler. I had forgotten, really, about The Beatles thing. Anyway, Billie Allen had said to me, "You've got to call up Nan Lanier when you're in London." Well I had never called Nan Lanier.

Nan Lanier was Tennessee Williams' cousin. She's my age. She was divorced . . . had been married to a minister in New York. I can't remember his name. Nan was one of the founders of the American Place Theatre. And Nan Lanier loved *Funnyhouse*. When I called her. She said, "Adrienne, I've been wondering how to find you." She said, "Billie told me that you're over here. Where do you live?" And I told her 35 Chalcot Crescent. And she said, "Well, we live right above you. We live in Hampstead. All you have to do is just walk up the hill and then turn the corner and there we are." By now it was summer. It was warm outside. So I took you and we walked up the hill . . . and there she was.

You see it was an atmosphere . . . She was an exile . . . She was divorced. She had children. All these people were running around her house. It was a huge house. You know, she's the rich American divorcee. You see there were so many people that were like me, people who were in London because London had this aura and they were coming to look for something.

She asked what I was doing. I told her I had these pages of a *Lennon Play* and that I had met once with Tom Maschler. And she said, "Oh, Adrienne. I can help you. Victor Spinetti. You know him. He was in both Beatle movies. *Help!* and *A Hard Day's*

Night." And this is just what she said, "He's my dearest friend and he knows The Beatles very well. I know he would love to work on a project like this." *(Laughs)* And we had just walked up the hill to say hello to her. There was something in the air, Adam. There really was something in the air . . .

Nan went to the phone and called him. He lived near Baker Street. She said, "He can't come over right now. But he wants you to come down to the theater to see him tomorrow. He's in *The Odd Couple* on Leicester Square." You know, the famous square where all the theaters are. You were in school. I don't think I took you, but I'm not sure.

So I went down to see Victor and he was excited. He said, "Nan says you have an adaptation of John Lennon's nonsense book. John is a friend of mine. What I'll do is I'll go out to" . . . I think they lived someplace called Weybridge . . . "I'll go out to Weybridge and talk to John. And I'll find out if he would like to work on something like this." I think he called John . . . he did! He called me up and he said, "I've called John and he's very interested in this." So Nan Lanier's all excited now. She calls to tell me that Victor's called up John and John is very interested.

In the meantime, Mother had brought Joedy from Washington. She was on her way to France. The very night that Mother was leaving she was going to get up at 3:30 A.M. and take the boat-train to France . . . I'll never forget . . . she was so excited. Ricki Huston, that very same night had these tickets to a reading. I asked Mother did she want to go. She said, "No. I'll stay here with Adam. You go, because I have to get up at 3:30 A.M. because I'm going to France." And she was like a teenager. She was so happy. She said, "I'm going to France!" She was going to meet Louise Kent and another friend in Paris. It was 1967. She was sixty. She was so excited. I'll never forget it.

Primrose Hill music begins.

That summer we used to go to Primrose Hill. That summer you played with Bobby and the girl from Kansas. She used to dress you up . . . you used to dress up and put on plays. It was the most enchanting thing. She was an American girl and she was from Kansas, her name was Dorothy. She used to dress you up in all these costumes and you used to put on plays out in the street. And her parents were so excited that she had an American child to play with.

So everything just seemed . . . wonderful. We went to Ricki's almost every Sunday; Ricki was a very intuitive person. She knew that when I came to London I only had a little money. She sensed it. She was just like that.

I'm sure she wouldn't have been surprised if I had gone back the next week.

That summer, Ricki had parties in her backyard. Well, it wasn't a backyard. It was a huge garden. That's where her son Tony kept his falcons. And there was a pond. That was the summer that James Fox drove us home in his purple Lotus.

I went to this reading with Ricki. It was on the river. And Ricki said, "Oh, there's Kenneth Tynan." Tynan was the most famous drama critic in the world at the time and his office at the National Theatre was next door to Laurence Olivier's. Also, Kenneth Tynan had pieces in the *New Yorker* constantly.

Primrose Hill music begins to fade.

I had never met him, but I had met his wife at Actors Studio once . . . his ex-wife. She was a playwright. We went over to say hello to him and he said he had never seen *Funnyhouse*, but Ellen Holly, who had a leading role was a friend. He asked what I was doing in London. I told him about The Beatles project and that Victor Spinetti had mentioned it to John Lennon. And *(Laughs)* he said, "Larry *[Olivier]* would like that." And he told me to come and see him tomorrow or maybe the day after.

I went by his office at the National and he said he had mentioned the project to Larry and Larry was very interested. Then he said Larry wasn't there right now, but he would like to meet me. And I'm thinking to myself *(Laughs)* Laurence Olivier, Heathcliff, wants to meet me. Here I am at the National Theatre, in the famous Old Vic, historic famous Old Vic . . . Laurence Olivier . . . Vivien Leigh and John Gielgud. I'm sitting in the National Theatre talking to Kenneth Tynan. You know me better than anyone else, Adam. You can imagine already what state I was in.

Tynan said he wanted Victor and me to come by in a few days. Nan played a big role in all this. Nan called up Victor and told him that Kenneth Tynan wanted us to come by his house. Tynan and Olivier ran the National Theatre, and running the National Theatre was like running England.

We went by Tynan's house. He lived in a place called Thurloe Square. As you go along, it is right beyond Harrods. He's right on the corner in this beautiful house. So now I'm inside of Kenneth Tynan's house, and all this is happening within the space of a couple of weeks. I'm in Kenneth Tynan's house with Victor Spinetti and we're having tea. We're sitting around having a conversation in his house. And he tells me in this stuttering voice . . . "I've told Larry about this and we've decided we want to do this. What we'll do first is we'll do a single performance of it, in December." He said, "Larry's very excited about this."

So Victor and I left his house. Now, Victor's been in zillions of plays, but he was excited.

ADAM

But you didn't have John Lennon's permission at that point?

ADRIENNE

John Lennon had told Victor that he was interested.

ADAM

He was interested, but he hadn't given his permission.

ADRIENNE

He had given his verbal permission. Lennon said he wanted to meet me. But nobody had asked John Lennon to sign anything at that point. I did sign a piece of paper much, much later.

ADAM

But you hadn't talked to him? This was all based on what Victor had said?

ADRIENNE

That's right. Totally. Victor went out there. As it turned out, only a handful of people in London could go out to Weybridge. This was a big, big deal. Victor had quite a niche with The Beatles. He had been in both *Help!* and *A Hard Day's Night.* John Lennon told Victor, "I want to meet Adrienne Kennedy."

Maybe a month or so passed. I'm not sure because I took you out of school that day. I think it was in September.

The Beatles theme music begins.

I kept you out of school so you could meet John Lennon. It was right off Piccadilly Circus. You and I and Victor went there. It was a very plain doorway, almost like a hidden doorway. We walked up these stairs and their studios were in the back of that. There was nothing about it grand or anything.

We walked up these stairs and there was this little room. We walked in and Paul McCartney was sitting on a desk. I'll never forget it. And he looked just like Paul McCartney. He was the only one, to me, who looked exactly like his photos . . . he had that shiny dark cap of hair. And he turned and smiled. And he was very friendly to Victor. Cordial, friendly, familiar. He had this quality. He just exuded this quality. Victor introduced me to him and he was very cordial, relaxed, very warm. And automatically he picked you up and put you on his lap and just started to talk to you. Don't ask me what he said to you. I have no idea.

The Beatles liked Black people. They had worked with Mary Wells. They were crazy about Chuck Berry, Little Richard. They had a real regard for Black music. There's been so much more written about it over the last twenty-five years.

The Beatles theme music begins to fade.

I think the only thing Paul asked me was if I was from New York. And I had a little postcard of Uccello's Mandolins, I think that's what it's called, and I asked him if he would sign it. That's the post-card that was stolen. He looked at it and laughed and signed it.

They talked about John. Paul put you down eventually, but Paul talked to you for quite a while. I don't know what he said. You can't manufacture that, Adam. He had a quality that just filled the room.

I think they said something like, "John is late." So we waited. I don't know if that was a minute or ten minutes. There were a couple of people in this office doing something. I have no idea what. Finally, Victor said, "I guess we should go."

Paul McCartney said, "He's late. When he comes he's not going to have time to talk to you at all." So we turned to go out of the door and just at that minute, here comes this skinny little guy with all this hair and glasses on, pale skin, and wearing an orange poplin jacket.

The Beatles theme music begins again.

Victor said, "There's John." And he had the same thing that Paul McCartney had. He just looked at us like we were so special. Victor said, "John, this is Adrienne." I just felt so wonderful. He said something like, "How ya doing?" And I said to him, "This is my son, Adam." And he said, "Hi, my son, Adam." And his eyes . . . he had these eyes that were blazing.

Victor said, "I told Adrienne that you were really interested." John had that really thick Liverpool accent. He said something like, "Yeah. That would be great." He said, "It is really nice to meet you." He had this quality. It was so unprepossessing, so unpretentious. It was like he was glad to meet us, when obviously you would expect it to be the other way around. It was just unbelievable. He was very thin and pale and his hair was hanging down. He looked like a genius. I'll never forget. He turned and looked at us and said something like, "Bye bye." He was nothing like that person that I had seen in The Beatle movies. He was just this thin pale guy with wispy hair and his granny glasses.

We went down the stairs. Victor said John was very excited about this. And I believed he was. I was just so excited. We got in a taxi. I didn't take taxis much in London, because the buses were so wonderful . . . so was the Underground. And we went to Ricki's and told her that I had met John Lennon. She was so excited. She had never met The Beatles. For some reason, they moved in this tiny circle. So now everybody was excited. I had met John Lennon. I had met Paul McCartney. *(Laughs)*

The Beatles theme music begins to fade.

I had come to London with less than five hundred dollars in my purse. Now I had a Guggenheim and lived on Chalcot Crescent. I saw Donald Sutherland. David Bailey, the famous fashion photographer, lived around the corner. You loved it. You absolutely loved it. And when Joedy came from Washington with Mother . . . he was just crazy about it.

So now I had met Laurence Olivier . . . no . . . I hadn't met Laurence Olivier yet. But now I knew Kenneth Tynan and Victor Spinetti. I had met John Lennon and Paul McCartney. I don't want to exaggerate it, but we'd met many people. You know that picture where you're playing the game and Joedy's walking on the sidewalk? You both have your vests on. That very Sunday we went to a luncheon at a writer's house in Hampstead. A Sunday literary lunch. We were invited everywhere and we met so many people. Peter Eyre, Elena Bonham Carter, William Gaskill, Edward Bond. We were invited everywhere . . . John and Margaretta Arden . . . Adrian Hamilton . . . Zakes Mokae.

Around November Sheila Scott-Wilkinson who had been in one performance of *Funnyhouse* at the Royal Court told me that she had been spending a lot of time with Jimmy Baldwin and his brother David. Baldwin was living somewhere near Chelsea and was feeling a little lonely and wouldn't it be a great idea if we gave a party for him. She mentioned it to Baldwin and he said he would be delighted. Ann and Carlton joined in.

Ram John Holder West Indian–style music begins to play.

The party was at our house. We bought cases of wine, cases of liquor, and made huge pans of spinach lasagna.

A friend insisted upon bringing his entire light show. A young musician named Ram John Holder said he'd bring his band. We rented chairs and tables from Harrods. People phoned and asked what to wear. We lit the house with candles. All came. Some even came early. The band came; the light show lit the whole room. People were excited. Then Baldwin came with his English publisher. He talked to people and people talked to him. As he left Baldwin said to me, "Think of me as your brother."

Ram John Holder West Indian–style music begins to fade.

ADAM

You had finished more pages?

ADRIENNE

I had about thirty-five pages of *The Lennon Play* . . . So where do I go from here? The next time I saw The Beatles? So now we'd met John and Paul. Then we didn't see them anymore. The play was supposed to be around early December 1967.

Waterloo Bridge theme music begins.

I believe Victor and I talked on the phone a couple of times, somewhere between September and December. I know we went once to Kenneth Tynan's office at the National Theatre. It was always for me an incredible experience . . . you took the Underground to Waterloo Station. Waterloo Station for me was . . . when I was a kid there was this movie called *The Waterloo Bridge*. It had Vivien Leigh and Robert Taylor. It was a World War II movie. And they met in the fog in Waterloo Station. And you know that Vivien Leigh had acted at the Old Vic and was Olivier's past wife.

For me to go from Primrose Hill and come up in Waterloo Station was so exciting. You come up and there's the Old Vic. It sits there all by itself. Victor and I went to Tynan's office.

Waterloo Bridge theme music begins to fade.

I remember he said, "Larry's not here today." Then at some point he said, "I'd like to be the dramaturg on this. We will do the play on Sunday night, in December. And then we're going to put it in our regular season in May." I was so excited. Their posters were all over London. I did end up with a poster. It was blue. I kept it for years. I think I lost it when we moved here.

Victor and I walked over to Harrods. We saw Natalie Wood shopping. We were supposed to start rehearsals. I don't remember the exact date. The rehearsal was going to start in November. We were going to rehearse for three weeks, and John Lennon said he was going to come to the first day of rehearsal.

An Olivier theme begins to play.

I arrived at the rehearsal at the Old Vic. I had on a brown woolen dress and brown boots. I'll never forget. And I had this very pretty coat. I'm sitting there at the rehearsal and in walks Laurence Olivier. He came and sat next to me and he was friendly. I just couldn't believe that Laurence Olivier was sitting next to me.

Victor did a scene and I saw that it was very different than what I had written. He came over and said, "Well, you know, I changed it." He said something like, "Ken and I have decided we'll write it with you."

I was dazed. I couldn't believe that I was sitting next to Laurence Olivier. And Laurence Olivier kept smiling at me. Then he left.

Laurence Olivier, I don't know how old he was then. He had gray hair. I guess the closest is like how he looked in *Marathon Man*. He had gray hair and he had on a dark suit with a vest.

So then up the stairs came John Lennon. He had on an overcoat. He had on a navy blue overcoat. He looked different. He looked very different. He looked like a Beatle. His hair was combed down. He had bangs, and he had his hands in his pockets. And I don't think he had on his glasses. He looked like John Lennon. He came across the floor and asked how I was doing.

He acknowledged me. He watched a little bit of the rehearsal, and then he said he had to go. He said he was going to come back. Then he went down the stairs and that was it. But he looked like John Lennon.

I was downstairs maybe for an hour later, and at the bottom of the stairs, in a foyer was Laurence Olivier. And I just went up to him and said, "I just can't believe that you're Laurence Olivier." And asked him for his autograph. I was in a daze.

The Oliver theme music begins to fade.

Then there was another rehearsal. I don't remember if I went. Victor told me that George Martin wanted to meet me. George Martin wants to take us to lunch. He was The Beatles' arranger. He wanted to do the music. I don't remember going upstairs that day to the rehearsal.

I had lunch with Ringo, John, George Martin and Victor in the pub next to the National Theatre. Victor said, "Ringo might want to do something on it, too. The Beatles might want to work on this." He said something like, "Larry met with John and he's discussed this."

There I was wearing my favorite brown dress. We met them down in the lobby and I walked down to the luncheon with Ringo. These Beatles, they had something. He had these bright eyes. And he wasn't much bigger than I was. We had walked down a few feet and he said something like, "This was a good idea, but it needs a lot of work."

He was very nice . . . a charm.

We went into the restaurant. I remember all these kids. They were called the Young Vic, were all in there and everyone was staring, of course.

We had this lunch to decide what the play should be. George Martin said he wanted to work on it and he wanted to add some music. He wanted to know what my ideas were. By this time, I was just too overwhelmed. They, George Martin, Ringo, Victor, John, were all sitting as close as we are now. I just retreated. I was just overwhelmed by it. So, I think we walked out to the street and they got in a car and they said goodbye. And I was just . . . it was too much. I went back to Primrose Hill.

Now I had met Ringo. Somewhere in there, before or after, Victor gave a party for his friend, George Harrison. He said, "I'm going to give a party for the cast of the Young Vic. These are some of the actors that are going to be in it and George is coming." This was an incredible sequence of events. This is maybe October.

Victor lived near Sherlock Holmes . . . near Baker Street. I arrived. I remember it was cold. It was a small apartment and all the kids from the Young Vic were there, and George and Patti came up the stairs. And, you know, Patti Harrison was one of the most beautiful women in the world. She was devastatingly beautiful. She was in the press every five seconds . . . British *Vogue*.

They came up the stairs. But they didn't come into the main room. George stayed in the hallway. There was a little room out there. Victor explained that George was shy and he didn't want to come in.

London party music begins to play. This music should be a montage of all the music and musicians mentioned earlier.

There was a little room off the foyer. Patti was in the foyer talking to people. So I went out to the little room and George was just standing there kind of off to the side. So I said to myself, "This is crazy. You're not going to say hello to George Harrison?" So I walked up to him and said, "I really love your music." He said, with a tiny voice, "Thank you. Thank you very much." You could tell he meant it. Then he just looked at me and I remember I just backed away from him, because I couldn't think of anything else to say to him. And he never came in the main room. He just stayed back in this little alcove. It was dark back there. He stayed back in there. Patti was in the foyer. And the way she dressed . . . I don't know . . . in Chanel or . . . there were several London designers who dressed all those people. But she was in British *Vogue* every month practically. So I went and said hello to her and she was very friendly. And she said it was nice to meet me. She's wearing this green chiffon flowing dress and green boots . . . she had blond hair with bangs.

And, again, I was just too overwhelmed. I left. It was just too much. And that was the only time I ever met George . . . his suit was pink. He had crumpled hair. He looked like an intellectual. He was so unpretentious. He didn't seem like his performing persona.

London party music begins to fade.

I don't think I went to any more rehearsals. I'm not sure. Actually, I did go to one more rehearsal that was on the stage at the Old Vic. So again, for me to walk into the Old Vic, and see a play that I had something to do with on the stage . . . where Olivier and Gielgud and Ralph Richardson and all these people have been, was just too much. John Lennon came to that. Paul McCartney came to that. They had on overcoats. And I talked to Paul McCartney for a second. He said something like, "This is a nice stage." He seemed genuinely excited.

We had one more meeting. We had one more meeting with John Lennon, Victor and Ken Tynan, up in Ken Tynan's office to, again, talk about what was going to happen. And that's when John Lennon was sitting next to me and he said he would be going to India in the spring. He wanted to know when the play was going to be. Tynan told him May or June, and he said he would be back by then. He established that he would not be able to have anything to do with the play but he would be back by then.

So at this meeting it was established that Ken Tynan was going to be the dramaturg; Victor was going to help me write it.

The Olivier theme music begins to play again. To Adrienne, Olivier should signify grandeur.

Everything seemed to be alright. When we went out of the office Ken Tynan said, "Larry wants to say goodbye to you." *(Emotional)* I went down and got in the car and Laurence Olivier came down and said goodbye to me.

ADAM

Was it like a death wish do you mean? Was he saying like goodbye as in forever?

ADRIENNE

(Still emotional) I don't know.

ADAM

Was he like Don Corleone or what? *(Laughs)*

ADRIENNE

Why do you laugh? I was little Adrienne from Cleveland and Laurence Olivier was coming down to say goodbye to me. That's how the British are. He was very nice.

ADAM

When you went to rehearsals, obviously the very first rehearsal, you said that you saw it was different.

ADRIENNE

I saw that Victor . . . I saw it was different.

The Olivier theme music begins to fade.

ADAM

Okay. That's what I'm trying to figure out. So when you went to the final rehearsal, the rehearsal that was on the stage, was it even more different?

ADRIENNE

No. No. No. It was pretty much the same.

ADAM

Okay. So at that point, half of what you had done . . . ?

ADRIENNE

Yes. Yes. It was clear Victor wanted to help write it . . .

ADAM

So Ken Tynan didn't . . . ?

ADRIENNE

No. No. He was just the dramaturg. And somewhere in there, John Lennon . . . I don't remember . . . did we do it in person? . . . There was a little piece of paper that I signed that said that if any royalties resulted from this, John Lennon got sixty percent, I got twenty percent, and Victor Spinetti got twenty percent. So everybody was happy, at least as far as I knew.

ADAM

Just from your speculation, do you think that once Victor realized that this was going to happen, do you think he went to John Lennon and said, "Would it be okay if I helped write this?"

ADRIENNE

I don't know. At the rehearsal he said, "I'm helping. I'm helping to write this." It seemed natural . . . that we'd be co-authors . . .

You laughed about Olivier. You see, I'm learning as I tell you this. Laurence Olivier was Mother's favorite actor. She was crazy about him. And I was crazy about him. I love his Heathcliff immensely, his Hamlet. So then, it seems to me that we had one more meeting at the National. Because that's the time John Lennon took Victor and me home in his car. He had this big black car and this chauffeur. John asked me if I wanted to play with the car telephone. He said you can talk to anybody in the world.

ADAM

He had a telephone in the car?

ADRIENNE

Yeah. You see, I can't explain how he was. There was nothing about him that was pompous. He said, "Do you want to play with the telephone?" I remember saying no.

He said we could all go out to lunch, but first he had to make a stop at someone's house. He wanted to see if anyone was home. He said, "I'll see if they're home. If they're not home, we can all go out to lunch." So he went up a flight of stone stairs and he came back. It was near Belgrave Square. He said they were home and he told his chauffeur to take us where we wanted to go.

So Victor and I were in a car with John Lennon's chauffeur. John always said things like "bye bye" or "toodle loo." He used "toodle loo" a lot. He said, "Toodle loo." And I hadn't heard "toodle loo" since my summers in Georgia. You know, so many Georgia expressions were British expressions.

The chauffeur took Victor home first, because Victor was near Baker Street. Then the chauffeur took me home and asked me for a date. *(Laughs)* He said, "Would you like to go out tonight?" *(Still laughing)* He was a huge guy. He looked to be Mediterranean, like a big boxer. Anyway, I don't want to get into analyzing it. But John Lennon made it very clear that he was very happy that he was going to have a play at the National Theatre based on his work. I remember he said in the office, "Maybe it will be running when I'm thirty." He actually said that.

ADAM

How old was he?

ADRIENNE

Well, he was born in 1940, and that was 1967. So how old would that make him?

ADAM

Twenty-seven.

ADRIENNE

He actually said that. He said, "Maybe it will be running when I'm thirty." And he laughed. That was the time when we were in Ken Tynan's office. And he had this tiny little laugh. He had a little high-pitched laugh.

For the Sunday evening, I had a special coat made. There was a young tailor. He used to always talk to me in Primrose Hill. He was about twenty-four years old. He and his wife were both designers and they had a little dressmaking shop right there on Regent's Park Road . . . it was a charming little dressmaking shop.

He was interested in my coats. He would say he could tell I was an American. He said, "Where did you buy that coat?" I had a gray coat. I bought it at Saks. He said it was a very pretty coat, based on the lines of Givenchy. And it was, because I used to try to . . . wear imitation Givenchy. He made this coat out of a tapestry and a skirt and a dark blue blouse. I kept it until I moved off of 79th Street. I wore it for years and years and years. When you went away to college, I lost track of it.

That night Victor told me he would be talking to the actors, running them through their final paces and I was supposed to have dinner with Laurence Olivier, Kenneth Tynan and Penelope and John Mortimer. John Mortimer, a writer, who wrote *Rumpole*, was a famous lawyer also. And his wife was a novelist and journalist. She wrote *The Pumpkin Eater*. I was supposed to have dinner with the Mortimers and Olivier and Tynan. So that's what I did. I can see now . . . I didn't really understand this . . . *(Emotional)* It's Olivier that makes me cry . . . I had dinner with Laurence Olivier sitting right next to me in a restaurant right next to the Old Vic. *(Wistful)* And I was just . . .

ADAM

So, in retrospect you said you were overwhelmed. Were you talking?

ADRIENNE

I was barely talking, Adam.

ADAM

I mean were you holding full-fledged conversations with these people?

ADRIENNE

No! I wasn't holding full-fledged conversations. I think they were saying things like, "We hope it goes well tonight."

. . . Adam, I was totally . . . fixed . . . on the fact that Laurence Olivier was sitting next to me. That's all I could think of . . . I said out loud . . . without meaning to, "I can't believe you're Laurence Olivier." . . . I could barely see the others . . . I only knew his arm was near mine. And that he glanced at me. He had on a jacket . . . a brownish tweed.

I think they had already decided that they were going to dump me. By the time of this dinner, they had decided that John Lennon was the author. And Victor was the director. And I understand later, from Victor, that Olivier had met with John Lennon maybe once or twice.

ADAM

Had they decided that they would keep your name on it?

ADRIENNE

They knew already that they wanted John Lennon to be the author. I don't know how to spell it out . . . you know, that's common in theater, movies too . . . you sort of keep somebody's name on it . . . but they had already decided that John Lennon was to be the author. They were going to deal with John Lennon from then on. I don't know how else to say it. They would keep my name somewhere there. They had already made up their minds about that.

So we had this dinner . . . Adam, you asked was I talking. I was considerably quiet in those days. I was quiet with everyone. I've talked more in the last twenty years than I've ever talked. I was a quiet person. So if I'm sitting eating dinner, whether it is Laurence Olivier or whoever, I'm not saying all that much. I was quiet. I've gotten more talkative . . . I mean, you're not a good person to judge this . . . I can hold casual conversations with people much better in the last twenty years as I've gotten older. I wasn't talking. But I did blurt out that one thing.

As I recall, Kenneth Tynan was very talkative. I would imagine . . . I don't remember . . . He would just be saying like "so and so and so . . ." And Olivier would just look at me. I don't know why. But he would just look at me.

As we walked down the street to go back to the theater, I'll never forget it, Sean Connery came along the street with Diane Cielento. And I remember Kenneth Tynan saying, "There's Sean Connery." Kenneth Tynan said something like, "John couldn't come to the dinner, but John's coming tonight."

Music plays, signifying the entrance into the theater.

As we went into the theater Kenneth Tynan disappeared . . . and the Mortimers disappeared . . . Laurence Olivier said to me, "We're going to sit together."

To get into the theater, we had had to pass by all these people. That's the first time this ever happened. I was on the red carpet. There were people behind velvet ropes. I'll never forget. Ann was behind the ropes, Ann Colcord. There were people behind the ropes. That's never happened, before or since. The ropes ran all the way upstairs. People were waiting to see Laurence Olivier and to see The Beatles. Laurence Olivier was holding my arm. I wish I had a picture of it. My friend Ann called out my name. Laurence Olivier led me to my seat. When the play started . . . I think I told you that . . . he took my hand.

Well you see, Adam. You can laugh if you want to . . . Adrienne from Cleveland . . . I was out of it. I could have had cut my head off . . . I was sitting next to Laurence Olivier . . . Laurence Olivier. There were people behind these gold ropes. There's my best friend in London behind a gold rope waving at me.

The music fades.

They had decided that I was expendable. And they were going to do it as gracefully as possible. I think somebody told me much later, Mike Weller, an American playwright. He said, "You weren't a major American writer. You weren't Norman Mailer. Yes. You had an OBIE, but they felt that they could gracefully do it."

John came in at the very end. That's when I really got the first sense that he was a Beatle. Because at the very end, right before the lights went down, he ran in with his wife, Cynthia. He ran in and he sat down in front. And all these people started whispering, "There's John Lennon. There's John Lennon." And all these celebrities were there. I don't know who they were. Sean Connery . . . I mean all these celebrities came to see this.

It was celebrities, celebrities, celebrities. All I knew was Laurence Olivier was holding my hand and he would look at me and smile.

When it was over, I don't remember anything about the play really, we went into the aisle, and walked down to the front. Kenneth Tynan was standing there. He said, "John left." Laurence Olivier turned and looked at me and said goodnight.

As I'm telling you this, it is very clear that Laurence Olivier was the most important person in this thing for me. He looked at me and he smiled and said goodnight. And I think Kenneth Tynan said, "Larry has to go back to the country," or something like that. And Tynan said, "Would you like to have dinner with us?"

But I was having dinner with the Hustons. They took me to a famous Italian restaurant. I don't know the name of it. I think a lot of movie stars went there.

It was Ricki, Tony, Anjelica. I was excited. I was working with The Beatles. There was going to be a play by the end of May or beginning of June . . . on the stage at the National Theatre. The cast would be the Young Vic.

ADAM

Were there reviews of this performance?

ADRIENNE

I don't know. The next morning I didn't hear from Victor. Victor used to call me up sometimes in the morning. I didn't hear from him and I was surprised I didn't hear from him. I remember exactly where I was sitting in the bedroom. The phone was downstairs in the bedroom. So I called him up at about ten or eleven o'clock.

He said, "I have something to tell you. John wants to be the author of this play. You'll have to discuss it with Tynan. Larry has met with him, and John wants to be the author. That's all I know.

You'll have to discuss it with Ken." And then he said, "What do you know about a Liverpool boy's childhood?"

I called Ken Tynan. He said, "I'm working on a deadline now. I can't talk to you." He said, "It has all been settled. John's going to work on this." And he hung up. So there I was. I was Adrienne Kennedy again.

I was crying . . . you know Joe Chaikin. Joe had been in London doing *America Hurrah*. And he had taken me over to Adrian Mitchell's house in Hampstead. Adrian, a very well-known poet, had worked on *Marat/Sade*. He and his wife and children lived near Nan Lanier.

I called him. I asked Adrian what I could do. He said, "I don't know. I don't know what you can do. You're not a member of any British writer's group. You don't have any recourse." He said he would ask John Mortimer what I should do. He said he would call me right back, and he did. He said, "I talked to John Mortimer and he said you really don't have much recourse. You did sign a paper for the Sunday night. But the contract you signed was only for the Sunday night."

Then Adrian called another friend. I think he wrote *Bedazzled* and was a part of *Beyond the Fringe*. Adrian said his friend lived near John Lennon in Weybridge. And maybe he could go over and talk to John and find out what happened. So Adrian called his friend and he went to see John.

Adrian called me back later that day. He said, "John's going to call you." The phone rang soon after. He said, "Adrienne, this is John. What's it all about?" And I told him they were going to kick me out of the project. I'll never forget. There was a silence. He said something like, "I'm sorry to hear that." I said, "They told me that you wanted to write it." He said, "I don't want to write it. I'm going to India next week, and I'm not coming back until May." He said, "I'm sorry to hear this." He was silent for a while, then he said, "Why don't we all meet in my office at Apple on Monday? I'll be in my office at Apple on Monday afternoon. You and Victor come by and we'll straighten all this out." I'll never forget. He said, "We'll clear the air." Then he said, "Toodle loo."

Victor called me up and said that John said we're supposed to meet at Apple. He said, "I'll meet you out in front." I think Apple was somewhere over there by Savile Row.

I met Victor out in front of Apple. You could tell Victor was very angry. We went up in the elevator and he said, "I don't know what you're doing." We got off the elevator. It was a crowded room. You could tell they were The Beatles. The room was just loaded with people doing things, lots of activity. Secretaries were just running around, lots of people. Apple was their headquarters.

A secretary told us that John would be right with us. A split second later, John comes out of this room. He looked at me and said, "We're going to straighten this out." He looked like he did the first time I met him. He had on his granny glasses. He didn't look like a Beatle. He did have these different personas. His hair was disheveled. He looked like a mad genius.

He led us into this little office, this tiny office. It was empty except for a desk and a couple of chairs. He said, "Victor, I don't want Adrienne Kennedy kicked out of this project. And I'm going to call up Ken Tynan while she's sitting here." He picked up the phone. He said, "I've told Tynan I was going to call him. I told him we were meeting."

He called up Ken Tynan. He said, "I want you to know that Adrienne Kennedy is here. Victor is here. I don't want her kicked out of this project. I'm going to India next week. I don't have time and I don't want to write it."

That went on for maybe three minutes. He walked us out to the lobby and said goodbye. I'll never forget how he looked. He looked like someone deep in another domain.

Victor and I went down in the elevator. Victor said goodbye. John was going to India for all those months. That was maybe December. So I kind of put it in the back of my mind. I knew we wouldn't be starting rehearsals until May. I thought it was all settled. In January, I looked forward to going to Paris to see *Funnyhouse of a Negro* at the Petit Odéon, directed by the great Jean-Marie Serreau, which we did.

I continued corresponding with Joe Papp about my play *Cities in Bezique* being at The Public in its second season.

The Beatles went to India. They were all over the papers. There was something called the *Daily Express*. I don't know when it was. Maybe it was in April. I felt secure. I got another Rockefeller Grant thanks to Henry Romney. Joe was still sending me alimony. I decided I would try to stick it out in London maybe another six months.

Ricki called me to have lunch. Then she asked me, "Why aren't you at the rehearsals?" She said, "The rehearsals of *The Lennon Play.*"

Knowing Ricki, that's why she invited me to lunch, to tell me. She said, "Well they've been rehearsing *The Lennon Play* for three weeks. My friend told me."

I talked to Adrian once more. He said there was nothing I could do. He said, "You don't belong to any British organization that can protect you. There's nothing you can do." And he encouraged me to let go of it. He's a wonderful person. He said, "Let go of it. They are tough guys." He knew them all well, so I just let go of it.

Elena Bonham Carter was a friend of mine. She was close friends with the woman who produced *Funnyhouse* in Boston, named Stephanie Sills. Stephanie had taken me over there when she had come to London.

Elena wanted to help. She thought I had such a very wonderful London life. We used to go over there.

Her home on West Heath with a circular drive had a romantic setting . . . paintings of ships . . . a tennis court. She got her lawyer. They were called Crawley and de Reya. I still have their letterhead somewhere. They were lawyers to royalty.

She asked him could he do anything. He looked into it and told her that there was nothing he could do.

So I decided to let go of it. They called me a few days before the play opened in June. A woman said, "Laurence Olivier and Ken Tynan would like to invite you to the opening of *The Lennon Play*." I couldn't believe it. "There'll be four tickets for you." On the same day someone else from the National called me and said they wanted me to know that they were going to put my name on the program and poster. I did not go to the play.

My mother sent me a dozen red roses on opening night. I had never told her that I had lost the project. She sent them to the National Theatre, London, England. They were delivered to me on Chalcot Crescent the next day.

I think the play closed quickly. Someone sent me the blue National Theatre poster.

And Joedy who loved The Beatles so much sent me a telegram from Sierra Leone. Even though he and Joe knew I had lost the project, they had an article about it put in the paper in Sierra Leone. Remember that little blue book, *In His Own Write*, had been Joedy's.

We were in London another fourteen months only briefly returning to New York for the opening of *Cities in Bezique* at The Public Theater.

Bill Gaskill was the head of the Royal Court. He gave teas. I believe they were on Tuesday afternoons. People I saw at those teas were John Osborne, Lord Snowdon, Jane Asher and Edward Bond. One of the best productions I ever saw there was *The Three Sisters* with Marianne Faithfull and *Early Morning* by Edward Bond with Peter Eyre. The Royal Court commissioned me to write my play *Sun* for their new theater called Upstairs at the Court.

Music begins to play. This music should convey Adrienne's release from London.

Ricki Huston was killed in an automobile accident early 1969. Late summer I packed our bags and came home. We arrived just as the Manson Murders occurred.

ADAM

And what is your reaction today?

ADRIENNE

I told it to you as honestly as I could . . . my search for fame and fortune.

END

Almost Eighty

At almost eighty, I wondered if I could find reasons to live.

I kept begging my son to print out pages of my mother's scrapbook, which was on his computer. Why?

All I knew was my eightieth birthday was in three months, and I was extremely sad. I had been at his family house in Virginia for a month, the month of June. For the first time I could not see how I was going to financially maintain my apartment in Manhattan, my beloved apartment on West 89th Street, an apartment I'd had for twenty-nine years, despite commuting to California and Boston, my precious home near the Hudson.

I seemed to lack energy, purpose. Dreams.

"Please print out mother's scrapbook," I begged. He was busy. The scrapbook was in the middle of other documents.

I didn't know why but I kept begging. I wanted to see that scrapbook, started in 1926. I wanted to see all the glued-on photographs and programs that filled the pages until 1928. And from 1928–1954 all the photographs and newspaper articles that were stuck inside the pages of the scrapbook.

I'd already decided if I can't find reasons to live, then what's the point?

What can I embark on at eighty?

What could I possibly embark on?

"Embarking" had always been one of my mental mainstays.

Finally, Adam printed out my mother's scrapbook that she started when she was a student at Atlanta University 1926–1928. I felt it was my compass. My beautiful compass.

The Crimson Cover

The crimson cover with a border of green-and-pink flowers started a long line of my love of books with red covers. Today I possess a small red library. As a child the sight of this red cover made my heart beat faster. I remember the twelve-year-old girl in Cleveland, Ohio, who held the book with the red cover in her lap and dreamed of life to come, dreamed of the future. I still needed to dream of the future.

The Red Book, 1943

Lying on the top of the book had been a long photograph of the graduation, 1928, from AU. The two-year normal school education made it possible for women to teach. My mother's first teaching job was in Florida, a white wooden-frame schoolhouse with about twenty children.

Then as I looked at my mother's fellow graduates, I thought of these Black women starting out on their teaching careers. A common thought was that the "race" had to be educated. Education was the only way for a Black person to compete in American Society. Could I still educate?

In 2011

At the beginning of the scrapbook, stuck inside a page, was the 1928 commencement program.

Commencement was a word I'd always liked.

Commencement
Commencement
Commencement

What commencement would I join? I didn't know. How can you begin when you're eighty? My father died at seventy, my mother at ninety-two, my brother at thirty-eight.

Fellowship

My father's Morehouse program was next to my mother's. Morehouse College, 1928, he majored in social work. Perhaps I could still look forward to *thinking* of that young social worker who left Atlanta for Dayton, Ohio, and then to Pittsburgh, Pennsylvania, where he worked for the K Clubs for boys, clubs formed to help youth in their goals, their problems, in overcoming the poverty they faced in 1929. The Clubs emphasized fellowship.

In 1929, fellowship was valued. I realized I could still look forward to *thinking* of these Negro boys in smoky Pittsburgh *and* my father and his young idealistic colleagues setting out to save the race. They sang at meetings:

> Blessed Fellowship
> Blessed Fellowship
> Leaning on the
> Everlasting Vine
> Blessed Fellowship
> Leaning on the
> Everlasting Vine

At seventy-nine, I still have the Everlasting Vine to lean on, and always will.

The original paper of the scrapbook is a pale beige heavy paper with a border of green leaves, green leaves to frame your thoughts. There is a forest of green leaves that surround this Virginia house that my son lives in with his family. I realize I can smell the soil, see different shades of green hedges along the stone path leading to the front entrance. Green leaves on this summer morning make me think of the green mint bushes we had in our backyard in Ohio and the taste of them in my mother's iced tea.

Green leaves make me think of the maple tree my father planted on the tree lawn of our house.

There is always a commencement of green leaves.

Lakes, Rivers, Streams

There is a photograph (1928) of my father in a lake sitting in a rowboat. He is wearing a white shirt and is somber. He is about twenty-four years old. He appears to be in the middle of a lake in Georgia.

Lakes. Lakes. How I love lakes. In Cleveland, we lived close to Lake Erie, the part of the lake that flowed between the shores of Cleveland to the shores of Canada. When I was thirteen, my neighbor took me on a cruise across Lake Erie to Canada. It was on a white boat, and my friend Rachel, her aunt, and I ate sandwiches and drank Coca-Cola. It was my first boat journey.

I had been on the lake in Aurora, Ohio, at camp. I had been in a rowboat on a lake with water lilies. Lakes. Rivers . . . The Hudson River, which I have loved since I first saw it in 1955 and have lived near since. My son's family lives near the James River.

Lakes, rivers, the streams that bordered the Faculty Club in Berkeley, California, where I lived often during the 1980s . . .

Even if I am almost eighty, I can still see Rivers. I can still quote Langston Hughes: "I've Known Rivers."

The Great Lakes

It made me happy that as a child I lived on the Great Lakes. Lake Huron, Lake Michigan, Lake Ontario, Lake Erie. I can still be inspired by the sound of the words and the pride I felt at being amid the Great Lakes. In Manhattan I can still walk to the Hudson, and in Virginia I can still walk along the banks of the James River in the sun.

In the Scrapbook

The words are written in Blue Ink.

Blue Ink
Ink Jar
Fountain Pens

I have a love for all three, there is a joy in looking at handwritten words in blue ink. We read blue ink, from ink jars in inkwells once upon a time. You filled your fountain pen with blue ink. I still have one fountain pen. A gift from Signature Theatre Company.

Aunt Rena

Rena Dickerson. She wasn't really my father's aunt but a woman in Atlanta who lived near Morehouse in the 1920s. She and her husband let Morehouse boys board at their house, and my father said she gave him and other students free meals, especially on Sundays.

I didn't meet her until I was twenty-two. She had long since left Atlanta, been widowed, and lived in New York in a brownstone with her cousins. However, she only lived in Brooklyn on her days off. Her regular job was as a cook on an estate in Greenwich, Connecticut. My husband Joe, our son Joseph, Jr., and I once in 1955 on a Sunday afternoon went to visit her in Greenwich. (At that time we lived at Columbia University in Bancroft for married students.) On that Sunday in 1955, Aunt Rena was buoyant, fashionable, and filled with information about New York City. She told me the only store I should shop at was Bloomingdale's.

But I first met Aunt Rena in 1954, a year earlier. That year, a new baby, back living at home in Cleveland with my parents. Joe was in Korea. Aunt Rena came to Cleveland to the World Series.

She got up at four o'clock in the morning to go down to the stadium to get in line for tickets. She practically ran along our sidewalk to me—amazing because I saw her as old. "How old is Aunt Rena?" I asked my mother . . .

Aunt Rena was so thrilled, energetic, and happy, had traveled from New York City to Cleveland. And the night before had made a gigantic pot of chicken and noodles.

"Rena's way up there," my mother said. "Rena's in her *late seventies.*"

Photographs

My parents in Atlanta when they were sweethearts.

They are standing near the steps of a brick home, she in a print silk dress with a pleated skirt. He has on a college sweater with an M (that I still have), knickers, and a baseball cap.

Silk dresses, prints with pleated skirts. When I was an adolescent in the 1940s, my mother picked out dresses for me with pleated skirts. She continued. The dress I wore for going away after my wedding was a shantung dress (she picked out) with a pleated skirt. She had continued.

Continuing (The Box Camera)

Until the 1960s when it vanished, my mother had a box camera that she had owned since the 1930s. She photographed rare events like visitors from Detroit or old friends from Akron, Ohio. These were people from their early days in Georgia, there was cousin Edith from Chicago. These people: cousin Hattie from Detroit, the Humberts from Akron, were born around 1900, came North to pursue tirelessly, relentlessly, and continually education, professions, racial equality.

Embarking on a journey was a theme that permeated my parents' and their friends' conversations. We've come a long way. We still have a long way to go. But we've come a long way.

They'd say, "I remember just four years ago we couldn't eat at Schrafft's in Downtown Cleveland. Before the War it was unheard of that Negroes would be living out here in Glenville."

Did I still have a long way to go? Maybe a long way to learn how to continue.

Scrapbooks

The red scrapbook, led to my own love of scrapbooks, love of photographs, passion for writing on pages in blue ink, writing thoughts on pages in blue ink about the days, events, the significance of a day.

I must continue to remember the significance of a day.

I think of: Morehouse College/History/ War Against _____

Martin Luther King, Jr., and his father, Daddy King, went to Morehouse College. Daddy King and my father were there at the same time. Martin Luther King, Jr., along with Nelson Mandela are leaders I admire beyond words . . . Purpose, fighting wars, struggle.

I must still be a part of the struggle. Perhaps history still needs me, so those before me won't be forgotten, obliterated.

Poring

I had published stories, plays, taught at UC Berkeley and Harvard; of course I had two sons by my only marriage and five grandchildren. But I could not see any future, a future with verve, hope, excitement that I'd once had.

I still wondered why I had begged Adam to print out the scrapbook. Why had I always pored over the pages, constantly gazed and imagined, curiously?

I realized poring curiously over pages was a trait I still possessed. I was still in possession of my curiosity.

In 2011

It's now clear to me that in her scrapbook my mother was gluing together a society, joining, adhering meaning.

Gazing and Imagining

1943 was the time at age twelve I climbed the steps of the attic in our house to sit on the floor, after I'd taken the red scrapbook out of the old dresser drawer. The attic smelled of furniture polish, old wallpaper, the old wardrobe trunk with drawers pulled out still with ancient gloves or a hat. There were broken dishes on an old chest of drawers. A small window faced the maple trees along the street. The floors were polished. The former family's grandmother had lived on this floor. I'd sit often in summer, gaze at the pages, and imagine ATLANTA.

At the same time, I started my own movie star scrapbook. In my movie star scrapbook, one of the pictures I studied again and again was a picture of Elizabeth Taylor in *Life* magazine. She was sitting in her bedroom in Hollywood. We were the same age, and I longed to be and to look like the little girl she played in *Jane Eyre*. Her name was Helen. When the cruel headmaster punished Jane Eyre, it was Helen who cried out in her defense, and it was Helen who was made to walk in the cold rainy courtyard of the Yorkshire, England, school with a weighted board on her shoulders. She died later that night. She had shown devotion and courage.

2011, this spring, I took out my scrapbook and gazed at the *Life* magazine photograph. I thought: I could still show devotion and courage. I could. I can. My family needs my devotion and courage, and for me to imagine a future with them.

On the back of the *Life* magazine pages were pictures of World War II in France. One of the great historical world struggles.

Gluing a Vision

I see one of the reasons I begged Adam to print out the scrapbook. I longed for the vision contained in the songs, the poems.

Invictus
Out of the night that covers me,
Black as the pit from pole to pole . . .

The Vision

. . . the romantic images, these two Atlanta students, young Negroes going North. The romantic girl who pasted programs, napkins, tickets, wrote: "I saw my sweetheart today."

She Glued Together: A Concrete Vision of a Wonderful World

The words:

Vespers
Eventide
Baccalaureate
Nearer My God to Thee
Salvation
She Walks in Beauty
Friendship
Fellowship
Jesus is my friend
He walks with me and He talks with me and He tells
    me I am His own
I shall pass this Way but once
Scripture
Morning Service
Heaven on Earth
Remembrance
The song "Throw Out the Lifeline"

Gluing a Story

The red book glued together a story, a vision of beauty, romance, friendship with the language of a nineteen-year-old girl.

. . . the romantic couple on the grass would one day quarrel, part, and fight bitterly over the questions surrounding the death of my brother, their only son.

In 1943. Climbing the steps of the attic I was seeking answers. I must still seek . . . "Vespers," "Eventide," "She Walks in Beauty." I must still seek "Throw Out the Lifeline."

In 1943

Alongside the red book, rolled up in the drawer, was my mother's diploma, from Fort Valley Boarding School.

Before Atlanta University, my mother had gone to boarding school. Her father sent her to the school.

Her mother was dead. She lived with her grandmother who worked away at Warm Springs, Georgia. And who my mother said was "mean to her." My grandfather, a white landowner, sent my mother to Fort Valley. On holidays the headmaster of the school invited her to his family's house. She told me she was lonely and sought refuge in books. Fort Valley School imitated English boarding schools in the content of lessons and, as well as they could, in the decoration of the interior of the school. Many or most of the books and furnishings were given to the school by wealthy whites, the population of the girls school was, of course, all "Negro."

My father was from the same Georgia town, Montezuma. My parents had known each other since they were children. He had been at Morehouse Academy since he was twelve. My grandmother, a servant, dreamed of him being "somebody." His father, who sold fruits and peanuts on incoming trains, had disappointed her. My father always had jobs at Morehouse, and my grandmother and her sister, also a servant in the same household (owners of a canning factory), sent my father clothes, dollars, food. People in the town said, "C. W. was going places." After the Academy he went on to Morehouse College. He was popular, played baseball, and wanted to "lift his race up." He majored in social work. Summers, Morehouse sent him to the tobacco fields in Connecticut to earn money, and he spent one summer at the New York School for Social Work in Manhattan. They were together a young teacher and a young social worker seeking the perfect and equal American Life. "Helping the Race was primary."

I see I can still seek the perfect life. They also sought God. I can still seek God.

After 1928, the photographs and newspaper clippings, momentos, continued, folded inside the red book. She continued recording *wonders*, parties, banquets, church events, school events, napkins from her bridge club meetings, poems from the *Cleveland Plain Dealer*, *and* I must *continue*.

—AK
Williamsburg, VA
June 2011

ADRIENNE KENNEDY has been a force in American theater since the early 1960s. She is a three-time Obie Award–winner for *Funnyhouse of a Negro* (1964), and both *June and Jean in Concert* and *Sleep Deprivation Chamber*, the latter which she co-authored with her son Adam P. Kennedy (1996). Her other plays include *The Owl Answers, A Movie Star Has to Star in Black and White*, and *A Rat's Mass*, among other plays and adaptations. She received an Obie Award for Lifetime Achievement in 2008. Among her other honors are the American Academy of Arts and Letters Award, a Guggenheim fellowship, an Anisfield-Wolf Book Award for Lifetime Achievement, and a Modern Language Association Honorary Fellow. Her plays are read and taught in universities all over the world. She has been a visiting professor at the University of California at Berkeley and Harvard University, among others, and has been commissioned by The Public Theater, The Royal Court, Juilliard, and by Jerome Robbins. Signature Theatre devoted its entire 1995–1996 season to her work. Ms. Kennedy was inducted into The Theater Hall of Fame in 2018. She is a recipient of the inaugural Tooth of Time Distinguished Career Award, established by The Bret Adams and Paul Reisch Foundation in 2019.

ADAM P. KENNEDY is a journalist, writer, and publisher. He was born in Rome, Italy; he grew up in New York City and London. He attended Manhattan Country School and Riverdale Country School, and graduated from Antioch College with a double major in Soviet Studies and Journalism. Adam has traveled extensively throughout Africa and Europe.

He is the founder and CEO of Chronicling Greatness, a company dedicated to profiling pioneers and veterans. He has interviewed more than two hundred veterans from World War II to Vietnam about their lives and service, including generals; Medal of Honor recipients; fighter pilot aces; and Cross, Silver, Bronze Star, and Purple Heart recipients.

He is the creator of the television shows *Africa/U.S.A.: The Connection* and *The World Connection*, "edu-tainment" programs for teens that aired on network television and PBS.

In 1996, Signature Theatre produced his autobiographical play *Sleep Deprivation Chamber*, co-authored with his mother. That year, the play received an Obie Award for Best New American Play.

Adam co-founded Abandon Entertainment, along with Karen Lauder and Marcus Ticotin, a television and movie company that produced the feature films *Oxygen* and *Scotland, PA*; and the made-for-TV movie on TNT *Thrill Seekers*.

Mom, How Did You Meet the Beatles?, co-authored with Adrienne Kennedy, launched The Public Lab Series at The Public Theater in New York City in 2008.

Adam is also co-host of the *America's Place in the World* podcast with general Tony Zinni, a retired Four-Star United States Marine Corps general, who served two combat tours in Vietnam, and is a former U.S. special envoy to Israel and the Palestinian authority.